TRAVELLERS' FRANCE

A guide to six major routes through France

Arthur Eperon is one of the most experienced and best known travel writers in Europe. Since leaving the RAF in 1945 he has worked as a journalist in various capacities often involving travel. He has concentrated on travel writing for the past twenty years and contributed to many publications including *The Times, Daily Telegraph, Sun, Woman's Own, Popular Motoring* and the *TV Times*. He has appeared on radio and television and for five years was closely involved in Thames Television's programme *Wish you were here*. He has an intimate and extensive knowledge of France and its food and wine, as a result of innumerable visits there over the last twenty-five years. In 1974 he won the Prix de Provinces de France, the annual French award for travel writing.

Travellers'

a guide to six major routes through France

Arthur Eperon

FRANCE

Introduction by John Carter
Maps and drawings by Ken Smith

Pan Original
Pan Books London and Sydney

Also by Arthur Eperon in Pan Books/BBC

Travellers' Italy
Travellers' Britain

How to use this book

Each page is divided into three columns.

The left-hand
column gives
you the road
numbers to
follow along the
route, the places
you will go
through and
towns or villages
which are worth
stopping at. The
distances are
given in
parentheses.

The middle column
recommends places to eat
and stay at.

The right-hand column
mentions points of historic,
architectural or scenic
interest about the area.

First published 1979 by Pan Books Ltd,
Cavaye Place, London SW10 9PG
8th printing (revised) 1981
new edition 1982
reprinted 1983
© Arthur Eperon 1979, 1982
Introduction © John Carter 1979
ISBN 0 330 26862 7
Printed in England by Chorley & Pickersgill Ltd, Leeds

Acknowledgements

My sincere thanks to many people who have helped me with *Travellers' France*, including Jean Roma, formerly Director of the French Government Tourist Office in London; René Bardy, now Director; Pauline Hallam, FGTO Director of Information; Michel Place of French Travel Service who knows so much about the hidden treasures of France; Jim Cuthbert of Cars Abroad and Canvas Holidays for practical advice over years; to Sealink, Townsend-Thoresen Ferries, Brittany Ferries and Hoverspeed, who have carried us so often across the Channel; to Frank and Nesta Bough who road-tested a route so sympathetically for the BBC *Holiday* programme and brought back most useful advice, and to my wife, travel writer Barbara Clegg, who has done so much driving, eating and drinking for me around France that she has to starve when she gets home to keep her figure. I don't bother. No one looks at mine.

Above all, thanks to readers for their comments on hotels, and restaurants. They may contradict each other sometimes but every comment, opinion and recommendation is extremely useful.

Arthur Eperon

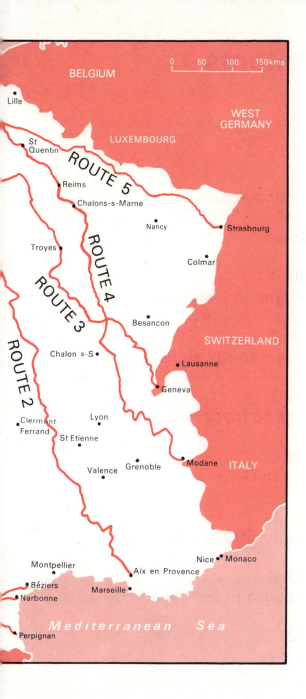

Contents

Introduction by John Carter

A week before I was due to deliver these words to the publisher, I met a man in a country pub-cum-hotel. He was one of a group gathered there for an annual dinner dance and, recognising me, paused to talk about holidays. (So what else is new?)

'Can't understand why you spend so much time telling people about these package deals,' he said eventually. 'Why not do something for those of us who don't go abroad on package holidays. Those who just sling the luggage in the back of the old motor and bomb down through France to the Mediterranean.'

I thought about that a lot afterwards. And if, like my chance acquaintance, you prefer to 'sling the luggage in the back of the old motor and bomb down through France', then I've got news for you.

You've bought the wrong book.

This book is for people who don't want to rush France. People who prefer to take it easy; to savour the pleasures of the neglected routes. To ease themselves gradually into a holiday mood, leaving the major roads, the autoroutes, to the rushers and the bustlers and the 'bombers through'. Let them go. Let them burst into France in a flurry of enthusiasm and recklessness. Let them hit the main highways and find themselves tucked behind the transcontinental freight lorries as well as the local camions, swallowing fumes and fretting about overtaking as they chide their front seat partners. Speeding through France is also one of

the quickest ways to get to the divorce court, so I've been told.

So let them go. Let them flicker over the speed limits and take the consequences as they worry about getting to their holiday destination on time. On time for what, for heaven's sake? The sun will presumably still be there, along with the beaches and the hotels, the camp sites and the restaurants. As far as I can tell, nobody wants to know 'What kept you?' when you are on one of those 'unpackaged holidays' and theoretically in charge of your own timetable. Why throw away the greatest benefit of such independence?

Holidays are meant to be enjoyed (oh, I know that is a cliché, but clichés often get it exactly right) and no way are you going to enjoy France if you take it at speed all the way.

So, if you are a 'bomber through', the only advice I can give is that you spend your money on car sickness remedies, pills for nervous stomachs and potions for tension headaches – or extra insurance. Chances are you'll need it.

Not just random chances, either: talk to anyone in the business who has to deal with holiday accident or injury insurance claims and the statistics prove the point.

Well over half of holiday accidents on French roads – accidents to British motorists, that is – are caused through anxiety and hurrying, and occur within 150 kilometres of the Channel ports. At the start of the holiday journey it is the anxiety to be on the way, to keep to some self-imposed schedule, to reach some spot on the map before nightfall. At the end of the journey, it is the anxiety to get to the port in time to catch the ferry home, having misjudged the time that should sensibly be allowed.

The map is such a temptation as far as the 'bomber through' is concerned. Tracing a planned fast route with the forefinger makes it all seem so easy as the kilometres roll away. The autoroutes and the major roads look so tempting, the challenge to cover long distances so irresistible. But resist it. Set yourself at most a daily quota of 400 kilometres – *not* 400 miles. Keep reminding yourself it is a holiday and not an endurance rally. And bear in mind, too, that in the summer the majority of road accidents in France occur on the autoroutes.

This isn't the place for me to go into all that advice about making sure you don't overload your car, and seeing that it is in good condition before you set out. But the 'bombers through' never seem to think about such things. They hit the motorways hell for leather and are surprised by mechanical troubles. A car which is well enough suited in Britain for a commuting run or a weekend trip to relatives just three hours away is likely to have problems if you try to carve through France. If you're in such a hurry, why not fly down in the first place?

Arthur Eperon and I have often talked about this book, and the philosophy behind it: the simple philosophy of trying to persuade holiday motorists that there is more to France than the Autoroute du Sud and that, even if you could 'bomb through' in comfort and total safety, you would miss the real enjoyment of France by doing so.

He knows France better than just well; knows it enough to acknowledge its bad points as well as its good, and enough to share his knowledge and his enjoyment of France with others – with you.

As far as he is concerned, the easy way through France, the 'spend most of the morning in the village market' way, the 'drive a five-mile detour to lunch at this restaurant and don't mind if lunch lasts until four in the afternoon' way, is the *only way to go*.

I have sampled France that way and much prefer it, although filming or working schedules have meant that most of my visits to France and most of my journeys through France have been conducted at too fast a pace for comfort. I have, of necessity, had to be one of those who 'bomb through' and cannot imagine how anyone could do that from choice.

So, please, try France the Eperon way next time you cross the Channel. With luck the Eperon philosophy will rub off on you. A philosophy best summed up by a remark he made to me when I met him after one of his many visits to that land he knows so well. 'Where exactly did you make for?' I asked.

'*Make for?*' he answered. 'My dear boy, I didn't *make for* anywhere. I was simply travelling through France.'

Preface

Instead of peering anxiously round the kitchen door, then hurrying back to his cooker, the patron of a small North French restaurant I have known for seventeen years stood relaxed and smiling behind his bar, wearing a suit and drinking champagne.

'Ah, I have been hoping that you would come soon,' he smiled. 'You must stay for dinner. Our cuisine is better than ever.'

'Have you got yourself a chef?' I asked, pointedly.

'No,' he whispered, 'a new wife. She's from Burgundy. She cooks even better than I do. You'll see.'

He was right. She certainly can cook. But what has become of France when a patron-chef will let a woman usurp his kitchen? Escoffier must be revolving in his grave!

Situations like that have persuaded me to write this whole new edition of *Travellers' France* after four years. Some restaurants have sold out at the top of the market, upped prices ahead of inflation or failed to cope with relays of hungry but critical Britons carrying *Travellers' France*; others have improved their décor, their bedrooms and service to cope with increased trade, hired new and better chefs – or even married new wives.

Routes are the same six travellers' routes across France, avoiding motorways but missing, too, very narrow roads where you will sit for miles behind farm

machinery. They are for travellers who enjoy France and want to explore a little, eat better and cheaper than in Mediterranean France and much better than in Spain. By taking them you will see interesting new things and places, enjoy beautiful scenery and unusual scenes, try new dishes and eat good meals cooked with expert care. France has all these treats in abundance. It is a land for the individualist who finds enjoyment in the world around him. As a bonus, on these routes he misses the chance of being in one of those motorway accidents which are becoming a scourge of Continental motoring, and avoids motorway exhaustion, a nervous condition recognised by Continental doctors, just as they recognise jet lag.

In many places I have suggested more things to see. It is hotels and restaurants which have had the full treatment – they have been rechecked, some dropped, all updated and new ones added. I have also put in days or weeks when each place closes. I did not realise before how many of my readers drive through France even in January and February. Or just how many families in France shut down their establishments at that time, presumably to join their British colleagues in the Tenerife sun.

Time was when a French *auberge* stayed in the same family for generations, shut only on Christmas Day. Papa went to market, then stayed in the kitchen, helped by his sons; the girls cleaned, sewed and served under the all-seeing eye of Mama, who sat behind the bar beside the cash till, cooking the books for the taxman.

Now they have accountants who advise them to sell out at the top of the market if a streak of publicity should bring the customers rolling in.

When Frank Bough and his wife Nesta road-tested this book on the BBC *Holiday* programme, they ate in the garden of a charming little hotel near the Dordogne, run by a young chef and his smiling wife. It was a very good meal in a lovely, happy setting. Readers flocked there. Then came rumblings of discontent. Had I ever *been* there? How could I praise the cooking? I soon found out what had happened. The owner, showing nice profits on his books, had sold out; the young chef had been forced to move to Bordeaux. The new owners were described to me by a French friend: 'They are *gentils*; they are *souriants*. Nothing is too much trouble. *Hélas*! He must be one of the worst cooks in France!'

But I don't think too many will be making their pile and selling out for a few years. The boom of 1980 will not be repeated yet awhile.

Overnight rooms cost money, of course. But taking things easier saves a lot of petrol, at higher French prices, and can often save an oil change. Have you ever looked at the colour of your oil after belting down a motorway all day? It also saves motorway tolls, which are now formidable, and if you are going to the Mediterranean it is highly unlikely that you will get a bed or a meal cheaper than in the hotels and restaurants which I have chosen – except, of course, cooking for yourself in a tent.

Most of the hotels, *auberges*, Logis and Relais mentioned are family-run. Prices are nearly all for a double-room without breakfast. There is a great shortage of single rooms on the Continent. Inflation has hit France as hard as it has hit us and hotel room prices have gone up in five years by about fifty per cent. But they are still some of the cheapest, cleanest, most presentable rooms in Europe. 60–80 Francs (£5.50–£7.25 approximately) is cheap for a room *for two people*. Similar British hotels charge about double. Continental-type breakfast costs 8–20F according to the type of establishment. The prices were correct as far as possible at late autumn 1982, but with inflation still rife throughout Europe and climbing in France, it is essential to check them before taking the room. Check also if they include taxes and service.

Always ask to see your room before taking it. This is normal in France, especially in smaller hotels, and wise in some because rooms can vary greatly in the same hotel. There may be twenty pretty, well-furnished bedrooms and a couple in the attic with junk furniture – let to latecomers when the others are full.

Tired, hungry and having broken my rule about driving too far in a day, I pulled up at a Relais with a log fire and checked-gingham tablecloths at seven o'clock one evening. They had just two rooms left, and other cars were pulling up, so we broke the other rule and hired the rooms without looking at them. The barman led us across the road to what looked like an abandoned warehouse. Up rickety stairs, along a bare rumpy corridor, we were led to doors which opened only after a battle with the key. Wallpaper stained with damp patches, worn rug on bare boards, wobbly washbasin and a huge bed with flashy-white linen greeted us.

The wc along the creaky corridor had no lock. I sang to repel invaders and, not surprisingly, received hisses. The plug pulled like a dambuster bomb scoring a direct hit.

Too late to worry. We went to dinner. The 40F menu was splendid value: old-fashioned rich sauces and large portions of fresh vegetables. The inclusive wine was so drinkable that we sank a couple of extra bottles as a soporific. After that I didn't really notice the tatty bedroom. All the same, I have not made the same mistake again.

Some readers, new to touring in France, have complained about hotel bedrooms, comparing them unfavourably with modern bedrooms of the Spanish 'filing-cabinet' resort hotels. True, you are more likely to get a *cabinet de toilette* (usually like a cupboard with washbasin and bidet) than a fully equipped bathroom and you may have to pay more for a bathroom. But most people going to France would plump for individuality, ambience and character above private plumbing and accept that in most French hotels under 3-star, kitchen and dining room take priority over bedrooms.

My heartfelt thanks, again, to many thousands of readers, who have written after following my routes. Sorry that I could not answer every letter, but the information has been most helpful. Most letters praised hotel and restaurant food. Many praised their welcome. A few complained, but usually about one particular establishment, whilst praising several others. I was perplexed by many complaints, because others had written in favour of the same hotels. One lady wrote a long letter of complaint about a hotel I mentioned. 'I was thinking of buying your book, but I am having second thoughts,' she wrote. Ah, well. . .

Many complaints were about hotels which had changed hands. A lot of these have been dropped.

Other new owners have settled in and give good value. But I think also that some Britons are expecting too much for their money – far more than they would expect at home.

Some do not realise that the French are people of habit, are punctual and do not eat dinner around midnight. One family sent me an indignant card from Spain saying that they had arrived at a little country inn in South West France at 9.30pm, had had some trouble rousing the management and that, when they came down from their rooms, the meal they got was not the real country cooking I had promised, but soup, a ham omelette and ice cream. It was off-season, and I reckon they were lucky to get a meal at all after 10pm.

Many French hotels do not hold rooms after 6 pm even if you have booked. Times are hard and they will not take the risk of someone not turning up if there is a cash-paying customer waiting at the desk. If you are going to arrive after 6pm, telephone ahead. Personally, I get to the night stop around 5pm, dump my bags and explore the district.

On the whole, French restaurants are still the best in the world and some family-run establishments are quite the best value, especially when the patron does the cooking and, just as important, the buying at market.

As in every country, meals have shot up in price. The increase is by about one third in four years. Usually, the old 30F meal costs 42–45F; the 45F meal costs about 60F. You won't find a better £5.50 meal in any other country. There are little inns still offering 22–28F menus, and those are often the places where they put a huge tureen of soup or terrine of pâté on the table to help yourself. Restaurants are legally bound to display their menus outside, including a menu *touristique*. A few restaurants who resent this cheap tourist menu offer a thin choice and small portions, but

mainly the meals are basic but good. Please don't expect gastronomic meals at tourist-menu prices. Some readers obviously do.

I have had a number of complaints about sauces and vegetables: 'a piece of chicken with lemon juice on it and two tiny carrots almost raw and a couple of tiny boiled potatoes', as one reader put it. That, ladies and gentlemen, is Nouvelle Cuisine, the new cooking, as interpreted by a lazy chef.

Nouvelle Cuisine came in a few years back with the fanatical French campaign for slimming and I am glad to report that among leading chefs it is already going out of fashion. It contradicts all classic French cooking which most of us love so much, and owes its temporary success to three factors – the French obsession with getting fit even when fit already, the approval of the French food guide of Gault Millau, which virtually condemns any old-style French sauce out of hand, and the support of lazy chefs who saw a way of saving time and trouble. It was intended to cut down calories by avoiding cream, flour and butter; if sauces are thickened at all, it is by reducing, and cottage cheese is used instead of cream. One good thing is that vegetables are cooked very lightly to retain flavour and crispness, but good French chefs did that already. Well done, the new cooking can be delicious (but not *all* the time); in sloppy kitchens it deterioriates into apricots or raspberry vinegar with everything and Pernod or lemon juice dressings. A French gourmet friend called it scathingly: 'Cuisine Anglaise – no sauces.' *Minceur* menus are for the genuine slimmer.

It was Clemenceau, not de Gaulle, who asked how you could govern a nation which produced so many cheeses, but de Gaulle would surely have issued a regulation against the current restaurant prices for cheese and the small portions sometimes offered. Even sadder is the demise of the great French breakfast of bottomless jugs of coffee, fresh hot croissants and rolls. Too often it is a cup and a half of coffee (which is much cheaper in France than here), frozen butter in silver paper, tiny pots of tasteless jam, grilled bread and a factory bun. If you get croissants, they are too often cold and hard. Honestly, I get better croissants from the baker in my neighbouring village than in some French hotels, though the French stick loaf is still unsurpassed.

What has pleased me more than anything is the number of French hotelkeepers and restaurateurs who have written fulsomely about their British guests. We are '*très gentils*'. Some have added in a rather surprised way that we are also '*très corrects*'. To be correct is important in France, and that, I am afraid, is where the few clashes have come – not understanding French manners. These are rigid and formal. In France, you *are* a guest– not 'the customer who is always right'. If you want to make friends in a French hotel, despite Agincourt and the EEC agricultural policy, you say 'good morning' or 'good evening' regularly, including to the waiter and chambermaid, and you shake hands with nearly everyone. You wait until you are shown to a table and do not just walk in and sit down. Whatever your schoolbooks say, you *never* call a waiter '*garçon*'; he is '*monsieur*'. And do not be surprised if the management gives a bigger welcome to regular customers than you. It is not race prejudice. The French love to see their friends. Use the same restaurant three times in succession and you will get the same treatment.

Don't be impatient if the waiter leaves a menu and does not come back for ten minutes. It is almost a compliment. He assumes that you are taking the menu seriously, as the French do. One French chef complained to me that it took him twelve hours to prepare and cook a four-course meal and that the British expected to eat it and be out of the restaurant in forty-five minutes, 'always as if they have to catch the last train'. Waiting between courses is inevitable if dishes are to be freshly cooked.

Then again, you cannot expect the same slickness of service from a small family-run *auberge* as from a heavily staffed, expensive group hotel. But you will be treated as a guest – a human being, rather than a room number.

Incidentally, the old story about the British being too shy to complain is now rubbish. The Consumers' Council, radio programmes and magazine articles have made us some of the quickest complainers in Europe. Some hotels believe that we are not happy until we have had a good moan.

In the routes I have given, you may be tempted to cut corners by avoiding some of the obvious diversions. That way, you may miss a lot. Gigondas and the Vaucluse hills look a bit off-track, for instance, in Route 2 to the Côte d'Azur. But this is a quiet, calm land unknown to any but connoisseurs of France. We went there first when wandering south to meet some dedicated mileage collectors in the South of France. A French wine expert had recommended Gigondas wine as the most underrated in France. A British importer had told us that it had a 'bouquet of manure'.

We found plenty of *caves* around Gigondas offering tastings – *dégustation* – and our tasting included swallowing. So we stayed that night at the Logis called Les Florets. Then we found the neighbouring village of Sablet *en fête* – streets packed with children's roundabouts and swings; colourful stalls selling jeans, toys, cheeses, wines and huge piles of vividly coloured sweets; children racing; women laughing; men drinking all round the square and a band with an age range of nine to seventy-five belting out marches.

There was a bull fight in which, through kindness or economy, the bull stayed very much alive, then an *aïoli* – 'a garlic' – at which 200 of us sat at benches in the village square and ate fish, meat and potatoes covered in garlic mayonnaise and lapped up litres of red wine drawn from barrels.

We danced in the square until nearly dawn to a group called Les Teddy Boys who could be heard several valleys away.

We were three days late meeting our friends – three days they had 'saved' to lie on a beach asleep.

I think that our holiday memories were better than theirs.

Reminders

Many restaurants have a special Sunday meal with a different price from weekdays. French families still take an almost ceremonial restaurant lunch on Sundays when they can afford it, and are ready to pay a little extra for good value.

Check the menu card outside to see if prices are 'Service, Taxe Compris' (STC) – service and VAT included. Some offer cheap menus *compris* but do not include service and VAT in advertised prices of dearer meals.

In the week, the French now eat between 12 noon and 2pm, and in some restaurants you cannot order lunch after 1.45pm.

You can follow the routes on the red Michelin maps (1cm to 10km). Some local road diversions are not on these maps, and although the signposts in France have improved enormously in the last few years, the local yellow Michelin sectional maps are not only useful for these few stretches but are also interesting. I find them well worth buying.

An important warning about road numbers: the French government, responsible for national roads, has handed over responsibility for many to the *départements*, leading to renumbering. The numbers on your maps may well be out of date. For instance, a road marked N99 on your map may now be the D999. It is not difficult to spot them, for usually they just have a '9', '6' or '3' added to the front or substituted for the first of three numbers.

Alas, some local authorities have not altered their signposts, so signposts along a road can read 'N23' in one village, 'D923' in the next.

French police now apply road laws strictly, and are much tougher about speeding than our police. Speed traps abound, fines are heavy for any breach of the law and are collected on the spot. So French drivers are more careful than they were and resent foreigners who are not (especially Belgians!). But they do not always keep to the 130kph (81mph) on the toll motorways unless they suspect that the police are about. Speed limits are 60kph (38mph) in town, 90kph (56mph) outside town, 130kph (81mph) on dual carriageways.

Parking laws are rigorously applied. The parking 'clock' system operates in most towns, so get yourself a 'clock' from a tobacconist and always prop it inside your windscreen with the time when you parked indicated. You may not park in front of post offices, police stations or hospitals. You must not cross an unbroken line, single or double, and you will be fined heavily if caught. Seatbelts are compulsory outside towns and children under ten may not travel in front seats.

You must have headlamps altered to dip left. French motorists also object if your beams are not yellow. Do both jobs by using yellow plastic lens converters or plastic stick-on strips with yellow paint provided.

The AA reminds us regularly that few Britons are used to driving more than 250 miles a day during the working year; 100 miles is enough for one stretch without a rest or walk. That applies to passengers as well as drivers, so switching drivers and pressing on does little to help you or your car.

Every year many Britons get into trouble abroad and lose a lot of money by not checking their insurance sufficiently. Legally you no longer need 'green card' insurance to drive in Common Market countries, nor in a host of others. Exceptions include Spain, Morocco and Turkey. But your own insurance policy will almost certainly give only third-party cover abroad and you may not be covered, for instance, against theft, damage or injury to passengers.

There are still such problems as getting help if the car breaks down or if a member of the party gets ill or is injured and such unexpected items as freighting spares from Britain (Continental garages do not usually carry spares for right-hand-drive cars, even their own makes), a hire car to continue a journey, hotel costs while awaiting repairs.

The nearest thing to comprehensive insurance is offered by the AA and RAC to members and by specialist brokers like Europ Assistance and Perry.

In EEC countries such as France you are entitled to the same medical treatment as insured nationals of the country. But do get form E111 before you go (you need booklet SA30 from your local social security office to tell you how to apply). I broke four bones in my back in France and ended up in Fréjus hospital. Hospital fees were £70 a day, plus consultant and x-ray charges. I had to pay a fifth of the hospital fees before I left. If I had not had the form, I should have had to pay the whole bill and waited to get the money back when I returned to Britain, after several weeks.

This also shows that it is worth taking out a personal medical insurance. A fifth of £70 a day, plus the other fees, is a considerable sum of money.

Ferries

Dover/Folkestone–Boulogne
(1hr 50mins – Sealink, P&O)

Dover/Folkestone–Calais
(1hr 15mins – 1hr 40mins – Sealink, Townsend)

Newhaven–Dieppe (4hrs – Sealink)

Portsmouth–Le Havre, Portsmouth–Cherbourg
(5½ and 4hrs – Townsend)

Southampton–Le Havre
(6½ and 8hrs – Townsend, P&O)

Southampton–Cherbourg (5hrs – Townsend)

Weymouth–Cherbourg (4hrs – Sealink)

Portsmouth–St Malo (8½hrs – Brittany Ferries)

Plymouth–Roscoff (6hrs – Brittany Ferries)

Ramsgate–Dunkirk (2½hrs – Sally Line)

Hovercraft: Dover–Boulogne/Calais (35mins)
(Hoverspeed – also from Ramsgate in summer – 40
mins)

Route 1
Boulogne to
Languedoc

This is an explorers' route and you could easily spend an enjoyable week on it. It avoids possible frustrations in cities and towns like Rouen, Le Mans, Tours, Poitiers, Limoges and Toulouse. You could miss out some of the more eccentric detours, but then you would miss some of the most charming places like Caudebec en Caux, Le Pin au Haras, Confolens, Brantôme, St Céré, Albi, a lot of fine scenery and good meals.

The new Brotonne bridge over the Seine at Caudebec, still not on all maps, is extremely useful. Crossing the Loire at Saumur not only avoids much tourist and commercial traffic but takes you to countryside and sights missed by most Châteaux of the Loire tours. The route through the Tarn to Carcassonne may add time, but it will also add an extra dimension to your holiday. It is beautiful.

Châteaux of the Dordogne and Lot are not so pretty as in the Loire, but were built by French or English for fighting and are historically more interesting. Their settings are superb. Quercy and the Lot area are as little known or crowded as the Dordogne of twenty-five years ago.

Even if you're making for Spain, it is worth a quick look at the Languedoc–Roussillon coast, almost literally remade with bulldozers – canals joining lagoons, marinas, big sandy beaches and new resorts such as St Cyprien, Port-Leucate, Canet-Plage specialising in water sports – but windy and coldish in winter.

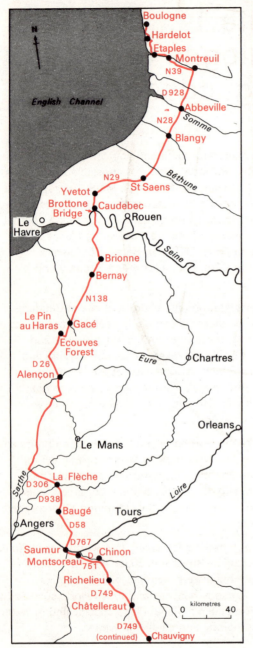

Boulogne
Hardelot
Etaples
Montreuil
N 39
D 928
Abbeville
Somme
N 28
Blangy
Béthune
N 29
St Saens
Yvetot
Brottone
Bridge
Caudebec
Rouen
Le
Havre
English Channel
Seine
Brionne
Bernay
N 138
Le Pin
au Haras
Gacé
Ecouves
Forest
D 26
Alençon
Eure
Chartres
Orleans
Le Mans
Sarthe
La Flèche
D 306
D 938
Baugé
Loire
Tours
D 58
Angers
D 767
Saumur
Montsoreau
D 751
Chinon
Richelieu
D 749
Châtelleraut
D 749
(continued)
Chauvigny

kilometres
0   40

Boulogne
PARIS
Béziers
Narbonne
Perpignan

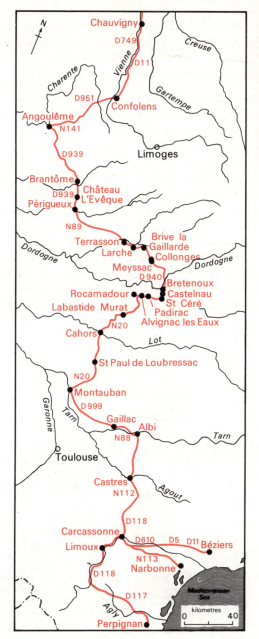

A trencherman's route this, with a wide choice of restaurants to suit different tastes and wallets. A route for those who like to take their legs from under the wheel frequently and stretch them under the table.

It's a butter-and-cream route, rather than an oil one. French cuisine is alive and well in Normandy, with good seafood, including shellfish, dairy products and beef. From the Seine to the Loire and Dordogne, freshwater fish – trout, salmon, eels – take over. The goose and duck are kings from the Loire to Toulouse, with such fungi as truffles, morilles and cèpes. The Loire meat is pork. Lamb is still dear in France and you get little local lamb until the Charentes around Angoulême – an area rich in dairy produce, pork, game, poultry, snails and particularly vegetables and fruit, including the Charentes melon. Vegetables of the Loire are excellent, even cabbage and especially tender broad beans. Fruit is even better. The food of Périgord and the Dordogne is rich and gorgeous.

In the Languedoc they cook in pork fat, although some oil is used on the coast. The pig and the goose rule most menus, with the haricot bean and more exotic vegetables such as pimentos and aubergines.

There are no really great wines produced on this route, but some good and some underestimated. Pouilly Fumé, that flinty white, is now dearer, but Pouilly-sur-Loire, using a different grape is very drinkable. So are the Sancerre fruity whites, Saumur white (slightly sweeter), Bourgueil red (nearly as good as Cahors), Chamigny red (lighter), Chavignol rosé (weakish, for hot weather), Layon (sweet, second to Sauternes). In Périgord, Bergerac has pleasant red, rosé and white wines (Rosette means white). Languedoc wines have been improved enormously by replanting, and good reds are Minervois and Fitou. Clairette is a drinkable white. Banyuls is sweet, heavy and heady.

Route 1
Boulogne to
Languedoc

Brasserie Alfred, place Dalton (21) 31.53.16: old wood, gingham tablecloths; still good cooking; deserved success means my old favourite has cramped tables, slower service. Menu 70, 150F (gastronomic). Wines good value. Shut Tuesdays.

Chez Jules, place Dalton (21) 31.54.12: younger locals eat here; plastic look – good value; try farandol boulonnaise (plate of various fish). Menu 53–60F. Snacks. Shuts 1–2am daily.

Chez Zizine, rue Amiral-Bruix (21) 31.43.24: looks tired, superb value for fish; small; many British supporters so book. Menu 40F. Shut Sundays.

La Charlotte, rue Doyen (next to 'Alfred'), (21) 30.13.08: tiny, enterprising cooking – try fish terrine; sole in mint. Menu 68–100F. Wines pricey. Shut Sundays.

Union de la Marine, boulevard Gambetta (21) 37.38.83: large, cheap, good value. Menu 30–50F. Wine 14F. Opposite fish market.

The port from which Caesar invaded Britain has stimulating vitality and is constantly invaded by British day-trippers until early evening. Good place for shopping, for cheaper meals. Fish market on quayside daily and food and flower market outside old St Nicolas Church in place Dalton Wednesday and Saturday 6am–1pm. On hill at end of Grande Rue is old Ville Haute, surrounded by 13th-century walls with seventeen towers. Walk round top of them for superb views; castle where future Napoleon III was imprisoned in 1840 after unsuccessful *coup* and Britain's Unknown Soldier lay in state in 1919 on way to Whitehall burial. Cathedral has a Roman crypt where England's Edward II married a French princess. Their son claimed the French throne and started the 100 Years' War.

Magnificent cathedral dome dominates Boulogne. From Gayette tower, de Rozier, first balloonist, tried to balloon

Club (formerly Hamiot) opposite fish market is no longer run by famous Hamiot family.

Le Ménéstrel, rue Bréquerecque (21) 36.60.16: good Relais Routiers; clean rooms, noisy street; good cooking, excellent value. Try fish soup, steak poivre. Menu 35–50F. Wines 19–48F. Rooms 50–60F. Shut December.

De la Plage, boulevard Sainte-Beuve (21) 31.45.35: friendly; useful overnight. Menu 50–60F; rooms 65–100F. Shut Mondays.

across Channel in 1785; he lies in nearby Wimille cemetery. Good shops, especially on rue Faidherbe and turnings off. Sandy beach where bathing started in 1789 has casino with indoor pool. If you support lost causes, see Napoleon's memorial to his army got together for his 'invasion' of England. (Off N1 Calais road – fine views from top.) On D940 Wimereux road see Calvair – huge cross dedicated to sailors.

Chapel (open) of nearby Château Souverain Moulin in Wimereux valley has three tapestries by great modern master Jean Lurçat.

Auchan hypermarket –2m on N42.

D119/D940 via Equihen Plage Hardelot (10km)

Du Golf, Hardelot (21) 32.71.04: golf clubhouse; smart, efficient. Menu 50–120F. Shut January; Sunday evenings, Mondays off season.

Hardelot Plage nearby is small beach resort with pricey villas along dunes, and pines.

Étaples/Le Touquet (22km)

Étaples – Lion d'Argent, place de Gaulle (21) 94.60.99: old-style inn already improved by young couple. Try moules; crêpes stuffed with fish. Value. Menu 38–99F. Rooms 60–80F. Shut Tuesdays off season.

Le Touquet – Serge Perard, rue Metz (21) 05.13.33: superb fish – own fish shop. Famous fish soup. Huge choice or 72F menu. Formidable shellfish platter.

Charlotte, rue St Jean (21) 05.32.11: new tiny bistro, fashionable with young. Menu 44–59F. Shut Thursdays; Jan.

Stella Plage (7km from Touquet) – Sables d'Or, ave Concorde (21) 94.75.22: happy, slightly nutty hotel by sand dunes; passable bedrooms, excellent cooking. Menu 43, 70, 75, 150F. Rooms 80–150F.

Étaples looks across the Canche estuary to Le Touquet but they are worlds apart. 1914–18 Tommies called it Eatapples. Fishermen sell their catches in quayside market; the square, with inns and shops, is chaotic fun.

Touquet is pricey, but a fine all-family resort – elegant again, with the rich in forest villas, Parisians and Britons staying by the beach in hotels or new flats. Lively shops, boutiques, bars, restaurants, night life Easter–September, then almost dead. Dunes, superb sands, horse-riding, ponies for children, show jumping; tennis courts include indoor with natural light; sand yacht racing where it was invented. Night clubs and discos. Beachside pool closed for rebuilding.

At Merlimont (10km): Bagatelle, famous pleasure park, zoo; great for children. (Open April–end September.)

N318 Montreuil sur Mer (13km)

Darnetal, place Darnetal (21) 06.04.87: one of my great favourites – happy, willing service; food better than ever; excellent coq au vin; fine duck with green peppers; delicious jugged hare (civet). Menu 46, 75, 120F. Shut Weds.

Like Rye, it has not been *sur mer* for centuries. Charming little place whose atmosphere grows on you; ramparts built by Francis I and Henry IV; tranquil old houses of the 17th–18th centuries. Napoleon's Marshal Ney set up HQ here

Central Hotel, Chez Edouard Restaurant, rue du Change (21) 06.10.33: simple, friendly; adequate bedrooms, good cooking; superb moules à l'Espagnoles; good sole dishes. Good value. Menu 49.50–65F or dish of day with dessert or cheese 38F. Rooms 75–140F. Shut 20 Dec.–20 Jan.

Château de Montreuil (21) 06.00.11: once 2-star Michelin hotel in lovely park, it lost both stars. Now Roux brothers from London's 3-star Michelin Le Gavroche run it, so soon all should be well. Pricey, of course – around 200F for a meal; rooms 220–330F. Shut December, Sun. evening, Mon. in winter.

At Inxent by D150 N to Estrée, then D127 (9km) – Auberge d'Inxent (21) 06.86.52: pretty, old cottage restaurant opposite old church; outside tables for summer; cosy inside. Excellent Norman cooking. Menu 60–100F. Shut Mon. evening, Tues.; 15 Sept.–15 Oct.

La Madeleine, 2km beside river Canche – Auberge du Vieux Logis (21) 06.10.92: rustic inn with menus changing daily; good value; try croûte of seafood with Armoricaine sauce. Menu 45–72F. Shut Mon. in winter.

for invading England. General Haig's HQ were here in 1916; Laurence Sterne began his 18th-century *Sentimental Journey* at the Hôtel de France, and announced that 'they order these things better in France' (he was talking of begging, not hotels). Faded mural in courtyard. Hotel needs refurbishing. Rampart walk under old trees round town (1hr) with superb views. Rose and white castle open except Mondays (push-button commentaries). Haig's statue; St Saulve church (13th–16th centuries). Market (Sat.). Lush surrounding country of pretty villages, meadows and trout streams – particularly along Canche valley, and also river Course (by D127 NE – superb run through sleepy villages).

Alternative route from Boulogne by D341 through Boulogne forest to Desvres, then D127 Estrée, D150 Montreuil.

**D113
alongside river
Canche to
Hesdin (23km)**

Brimeux (across river on N39) – La Toque Blanche (21) 06.10.09: new owners building up reputation to rival that of Mme Couchoux, here for so long. Lovely old house with big garden, but no longer offers rooms. Menu 45, 65, 87F. Good wine selection.

Hesdin – La Chope, rue d'Arras (21) 06.82.73: not much to look at, but just try Mme Samper-Deman's cooking! Mostly Flemish, but something from all France. Nice choice of cheaper wines. Happy, old-style *auberge*. Clean rooms. Menu 42–90F. Rooms 81–111F. Shut Thurs. except July, August.

Des Flandres, rue d'Arras (21) 06.80.21: modernised Logis; local businessmen use restaurant. I had superb Canche trout. Menu 40–82F. Rooms 47–160F.

Attractive old town at meeting of two rivers, with Renaissance church and pleasant market square. Town hall former palace of Marie of Hungary, sister of Charles V, in 16th century; ballroom now a theatre. Lovely forest (north); picnic tables. Just off D928 to north is Azincourt – which we call Agincourt – where Henry V with his small exhausted English army, racked with sickness, defeated the French army three times its size. Marked simply but poignantly by a cross over French communal graves.

**D928
Abbeville
(35km)**

Condé, pl de la Libération (22) 24.06.33: unexciting but good value; good local cuisine. Menu 42–75F. Rooms 51–75F. Closed Sun. and August.

Jean Bart, rue Ste Catherine (22) 24.21.71: modern, simple; recommended to me for good value; I have not tried it. Menu 40–80F (try ficelle-pancakes); rooms 50–120F.

Just to the right of the road is Crécy forest and the battlefield of 1346 where 20,000 French fell, mostly to English archers.

Moulin Eduard III, English HQ, replaced by flagstaff; views. Château de Bagatelle off N1 is a charming folly built by an 18th-century manufacturer to entertain business contacts.

Chalet, ave Gare (22)
24.21.57: remarkably cheap;
attractive. Patron-chef. Menu
27, 32, 48F. Wine from 16F.
Rooms 40–100F. Shut
Sundays except high
summer.

Au Chateaubriand, rue
Lingers (22) 24.08.23: I am
told it has good cooking and
choice. Menu 42–75F. Shut
Mondays.

Magnificent decorations,
including a fine staircase and
Louis XV and XVI furniture;
French-style garden within
English-style park.

N28 Huppy,
Blangy sur
Bresle (25km)
N28 then N29
St Saens
(44km)

In château at Huppy young
Col Charles de Gaulle set up
HQ in May 1940 for an heroic
counter-attack on Nazis.

The road skirts Eawy forest,
finest beech forest in France;
before St Saens, turn right to
drive down magnificent
avenue called Allée des
Limousins for a way (it is
22km long and was cut as a
fire break).

N29 Yvetot
(42km)

Market town. Church (St
Pierre) is a modern round
building with huge stained-
glass windows by Max
Ingrand defining the walls of
the belfry with brilliant use of
colour. From 1392 until
Revolution a tax-free
independent town.

D131 Caudebec en Caux (12km)

La Marine (35) 96.20.11: no longer owned by the famous Maurice Lalonde. Not visited since change. Menu now 120–150F. Wines from 70F; rooms 95–190F.

At Villequier (3km from Caudebec) – Grand Sapin (35) 96.11.56: Gerard Octau, chef here for twenty years, now patron; cooking better than ever. Charming garden overlooking Seine; simple bedrooms, sophisticated cuisine; try scallops; guinea fowl; snails en profiterolles. Meals 38, 65, 95F. Rooms 55–81F. Shut Weds. in winter.

France (35) 96.13.66: tiny, very simple; friendly. Beside river. Menu 49–75F. Rooms 85F.

Domaine de Villequier (35) 96.10.12: Maurice Lalonde, master-hotelkeeper, has finally left the Marine at Caudebec to settle in this lovely old house in a lovely park with views to the Seine. Pricey, of course, but a delight. All M. Lalonde's great duck dishes and his trout pâté survive. Menu 100–120F includes wine; 150–200F gastronomic. Rooms 180–320F.

Once an important place for crossing the Seine by ferry, it was destroyed in 1944 but the modern version has matured into a pleasant small town, with big ships passing its quays. Fewer lorries since Brotonne bridge was built, but still some. Henry IV called the 14th-century church of Notre-Dame 'the most beautiful chapel in the kingdom'. At Villequier, riverside beauty spot backed by woods, Victor Hugo's daughter and her husband were drowned. Victor Hugo museum is not exciting.

Over the new Brotonne bridge (cars 10F toll) then through Brotonne forest D40, D94, D144, D47, D130 to Brionne (45km)

Logis de Brionne, place St Denis (32) 44.81.73: high-grade Logis de France; reliable cuisine du marché – fresh seasonal food, so menus change. Good game and duck dishes. Good wine list. Menu 40–85F. Rooms 60–120F. Shut Sunday evening, Monday lunch.

Brionne built on islands where river Risle divides. Bec Hellouin (6km on N318, D39) was where the Italian Lanfranc studied. Remember him from school history? William the Conqueror had him made Archbishop of Canterbury and virtual ruler of England when William was warring in Normandy. Another Italian Bec graduate, Anselm, followed him.

Abbey (shut Tuesdays) was restored in 1948. From the remaining tower of the old abbey church are good views over Bec valley. Worth a detour. Château d'Harcourt (7km along D26, D137), cradle of a famous family, now belongs to the Ministry of Agriculture, has a park planted with rare trees, all labelled.

N138 Bernay (15km)

Angleterre et Cheval Blanc, rue de Gaulle (32) 43.12.59: comfortable hotel, good restaurant. Jean Cabourg patron-chef since 1948. Try trout, guinea fowl, fish. Much farm produce. Menu 66–170F. Rooms 70–99F.

Market town where rivers meet, known for cattle and horse sales; its abbey, where the troubadour Alexandre de Bernay invented twelve-syllable Alexandrine verse, is now the town hall; in the old abbey lodge is a really fine collection of pottery of Nevers, Rouen and Strasbourg, and period furniture of Normandy; interesting even to museum yawners.

**N138 Gacé
(57km)**

Hostellerie les Champs, route
d'Alençon (33) 35.51.45: fine
old house with park-garden;
swimming pool; period
décor. Nice atmosphere,
friendly service. Norman
cooking; lovely fish mousse,
fine cheese platter. Menu 60–
90F. Rooms 70–200F. Shut
Tues. low-season, mid Jan–
mid Feb.

**N138, N24b Le
Pin au Haras
(20km)**

National stud in courtyard of
an attractive 1716 château.
Magnificent horses include
100 stallions, many from
England or Ireland. Its most
famous horse, Furioso, came
from England in 1946. He
died in 1967, having sired
many showjumping
champions including one
Olympic and one world
champion, both ridden by P.
Jonquères d'Oriola. The
Queen visited the stud in
1967.

N24b, then D26
Ô castle
(12km)

Restaurant Ferme d'Ô (33) 35.35.27: attached to castle. Very good value. Menu 50F (not weekends), 75, 110F. Shut Sun. eve.; Wed.

Renaissance to 18th-century castle, prettily reflected in its moat; you can now visit inside and grounds every afternoon except Tues. Fragile beauty in its pointed towers.

D26 Écouves
forest to
Alençon
(30km)

Au Petit Vatel, pl Cdt-Desmeulles (33) 26.23.78: gourmand's 'petit paradis'. Pricey but worth every franc. Balzac wrote often of Alençon's gourmands and chef Michel Larat, now also patron, preserves tradition. Regional dishes, plus modern inventions like mussels in spinach, peppered lamb, snails in mustard sauce. Everything meticulous, from fresh vegetables perfectly cooked to wide choice of sorbets. Menu 85–118F. Shut 15–31 Aug., Feb.

3km E on N138 – Château de Maleffre (33) 31.82.78: lovely château in parkland with lake. True retreat. Rooms 65–180F; eat with the family. Mon.–Thurs. evening only, 80F.

Forest of mixed trees with deer and wild boar; glades for picnics and good place to stretch your legs. Here French tanks under General Leclerc defeated Nazi panzers in 1944 and at Carrefour de la Croix de Medavy stands a memorial tank.

Alençon, market town on the Sarthe river, is famous for 'point d'Alençon' lace started in the 17th century to stop ladies of the court importing lace from Venice. You can see it in Museum de Peinture and École Dentellière (lace school) but not see it being made. Many lovely buildings, including the Préfecture, 17th-century palace of the Guise family. Notre-Dame Church, 14th-century Flamboyant, has magnificent stained-glass and a very flamboyant porch. Town has good open-air swimming pool.

N138 towards Le Mans but turning right on D310, D4 to Sablé-sur-Sarthe, then D306 to La Flèche (98km)

Solesmes, 4km from Sablé – Grand Hotel (43) 95.45.10: extraordinary building opposite abbey – elegant old front, modern rear with round brick balconies like airy fortress. Very comfortable rooms; good cooking; huge modern kitchen you can visit. Try duck rillettes, pigeon breasts, chicken pot-roast in wine. Menu 60–85F; rooms 120–170F. Rest. shut Sun. evening.

La Flèche – Le Vert Galant, Grande Rue (43) 94.00.51: charming 'town house', prettily decorated and furnished. Regional cooking of local products. Good value. Menu 40–100F. Rooms 44–100F. Shut Friday.

Relais Henry IV on N23, 2km N (43) 94.07.10: Logis known for regional cooking; big range from cheap good value menus to fine gastronomic dishes. Menu 40–105F; rooms 53–85F. Shut Mon. evenings, Tuesdays. Meals praised by readers; rooms and service criticised.

Sablé is prettily sited on both river banks where two tributaries flow in.

4km NE – Solesmes Abbey; historic, now known for the Gregorian chant.

La Flèche – little-known town attractively placed on the river Loir (note: no e), it grew from a castle in the middle of the river. Henry IV gave his château to the Jesuits but it is now a prep school for military academics, thanks to Napoleon. Little town with old streets and houses and an historic hospital pharmacy with old bottles.

D938 through woods to Baugé (15km) D58 through forest of Chanelais to Vernantes, then D767 to Saumur (40km)

Gambetta, rue Gambetta (41) 51.11.13: best value meals in Saumur. Local wines include red Champigny, Menu 45, 80, 110F. Shut Sun. evening, Monday.

This woodland route to Saumur is nicer than the main road. A Huguenot stronghold, Saumur is now known for wine, religious medals and its cavalry school. The spectacular Louis X 14th-century castle on a sheer cliff, with lovely views,

Hotel de la Gare, facing station (41) 50.34.24: something for everyone: dish of day 18F; menu 35–110F; rooms 50–170F. Views of Loire and castle. Open April–end Oct.

Budan, quai Carnot (41) 51.28.76: solid comfort overlooking Loire. Solid meals. I have never eaten badly here. Good wine list. Try fried ablette (small river fish), river fish terrine, wood-grilled local salmon. Menu 70F. Rooms 180–228F. Shut 1 Nov.–31 March.

At Les Rosiers (15km on N152), pretty spot – Val de Loire (41) 51.80.30: informal, rustic, fun. Good value meals; good desserts. Menu 38–76F. Rooms 62–140F. Shut Mon. and October.

Jeanne de Laval (41) 51.80.17: Albert Augereau's lovely old inn and manor has a remarkable ceramics museum and a unique museum of the horse.

The cavalry and armoured school was started in 1763 when the best horsemen in France were sent there. The Black Squadron still gives horse and tank displays. Fine tapestries in Notre-Dame Church, better ones in Hospices Jeanne Delanoue. Jardin des Plantes – a series of flowered terraces down the castle slope, garlanded with vines, is delightful. At St Hilaire St Florent, a Saumur suburb where rivers meet, you can taste the fruity white wine of Saumur at the firm of Ackerman. Laurance Ackerman, an Alsatian, taught the locals to put in the sparkle by the champagne method in 1811 and it is a pleasant drink brut or demi-sec, though no substitute for champagne. The still wine, a

Saumur
continued

house annexe were chosen by the Queen Mother for her 1981 stay. I don't blame her. Really splendid cooking – well worth the prices. Menu 110–180F. Rooms 130–250F. Shut. Mon. Tues. lunch.

fine apéritif, is being made more extensively now and I like it. (Visits 9.30–11.30, 15.00–17.00, 1 May–30 September.)

**D751
Montsoreau
(12km)**

Hotel Bussy, Restaurant Diane de Méridor (45) 51.70.18: view of castle and Loire; simple; period furniture; rightly proud of its Loire fish dishes. Menu 51–85F. Rooms 48–170F. Shut Tuesdays.

5km before Chinon, 1km right on D759 at La Roche-Clermault – Auberge du Haut-Clos (47) 95.94.50: rustic Logis, modern annexe; good views; attractive; cooking over huge log fire. Menu 39–93F. Cheap red housewine. Rooms 45–140F. Shut Fri. off-season; Jan., Feb.

Château of Montsoreau, pretty and impressive, built by Charles VII's steward in the 15th century, in Gothic running into Renaissance style. A Moroccan museum inside. Napoleon made it a prison and it remained so until 1963. Fontevrault Abbey (4km down N147), built in 1099, had an abbess in charge, which annoyed some male chauvinist monks. The fine church (1119) contains the tombs of Plantagenets, including our Henry II, his wife Eleanor, their son Richard Coeur de Lion and King John's wife Isabelle. We tried to con the French into sending them to Westminster Abbey, but it did not work. Abbey kitchen is ornately photogenic.

**D751 D749 left
Chinon (17km)**

Auberge St Jean, rue St Jean (47) 93.09.29: Auberge Rurale, specialises in cooking with Chinon wine (meat, fish, dessert). Menu 35–90F. Small cheap hotel opposite.

Hostellerie Gargantua, rue Haute St Maurice (47) 93.04.71: in turreted 15th-century palace. Try Loire fish

A near surfeit of history in this delightful town. Rabelais was probably born here, Richelieu owned it, our Henry II died in the castle, then called Castle of St George. His son, Richard Lionheart, held it, but King John lost it to the French. Charles VII moved the French court here, listened to Joan of Arc's

and eels; locals praise cooking. Wide choice of wines include local Burgueil. Menu 79–105F. Rooms 90–200F. Shut Feb.

Château de Marcay (7km on D749, D116) (47) 93.03.47: in magnificent château; very pricey. Imaginative cuisine, à la carte only: 120–160F. Try duck pie, cold bouillabaisse 'en gelée'. Rooms 230–530F. Heated pool. Shut Jan., Feb.

strange story, believed her and gave her an army. The château, partly ruined, is still magnificent (Joan of Arc museum).

Old town of alleys and turreted houses – rue Voltaire and Grand Carroi outstanding.

D751, D749
Richelieu
(20km)

Le Faisan, place du Marché (47) 58.10.03: simple Logis; try river eels in wine; coq au Chinon; meals 38–80F. Rooms 56–140F. Shut Dec., Jan., Feb.

First planned town in France – by Richelieu. His château has gone, but the beautiful park is open.

**D749
Châtelleraut
and Chauvigny
(58km)**

Châtelleraut has good museum of old cars (including steam and electric) and early bikes, trikes and motorbikes. Across attractive Vienne valley, Chauvigny is in a fine dominating position on the Vienne; ruins of five castles.

**D749, D11,
N729, D951
Confolens
(76km)**

Auberge Belle Étoile (151 bis road to Angoulême) (45) 84.02.35: favourite of many satisfied readers for its friendliness, cooking, good value. Splendid trout. Riverside garden. Menu 40–75F. Wines 13–150F. bottle. Rooms 68–118F. Shut Mon. off-season; Oct.

Grand Hotel, pl. des Halles (45) 95.47.95: nice building, gorgeous gardens, fine views. Very nice hotel. Menu 70–90F. Rooms 160–225F.

Confolens is a quiet old town on Vienne river where it meets the fast-flowing Goire, with old houses between them. Most photogenic street is rue des Francs-Macons (Freemasons), with steps lined with overhanging houses. Fine 15th-century bridge crosses Vienne river to the 11th-century church of St Barthélemy.

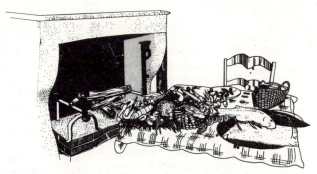

D951, N141
Angoulême
(63km)

Chez James, rue Genève (45) 95.18.16: restaurant liked locally; choice of cheap menus and gourmet à la carte dishes. Try confit of duck; profiterolles. Menu 35–65F.

La Marmite de Pêcheur (4km on D72 at Pont de Bassau) (49) 95.28.65: Madame Poupelain chooses ingredients and cooks them with the same care and flair. Genuine but smart country auberge specialising in genuine Charente dishes like eel stew, river-fish soup, farée (a filling, stuffed cabbage); spit-roast farm chickens; 'des bouchoteurs' proved to be 'of the mussel farmers', so 'mouclade des bouchoteurs' was a splendid creamy gourmet version of moules marinières. Superb sole; lovely goat's cheese. Menu 39–95F; middle-priced menus are outstanding value; remarkable collection of wines from 22F (Bordeaux); huge selection of champagne and brandy; shut Mondays and early January.

A pleasant walk round the boulevards replacing the old ramparts gives fine views of river Charente. At Promenade Beaulieu, overlooking Jardin Vert, is a plaque to France's first 'para', General Resnier. In 1806, aged 73, he invented a wing-flapping machine and took off from this spot. He hoped to have found a way for Napoleon's troops to invade England. He landed in the river.

**D939
Brantôme
(58km)**

At Vieux Mareuil, 17km before Brantôme – Auberge de l'Etang Bleu (53) 56.62.63: good service, comfortable rooms. Menu 65–165F. Rooms 125–140F.

Auberge du Soir, rue Georges Saumande (53) 05.82.93: attractive simple Auberge Rurale; good value cheap menu, good gastronomic. Menu 38–120F. Rooms 80F. Shut Jan.

Moulin de l'Abbaye (53) 05.80.20: superb conversion by Regis and Catherine Bulot-Benoist of old picturesque riverside mill into 4-star hotel. Romantic, beautifully furnished; inevitably expensive. Mostly Perigordian cooking. Menu 75–165F. Rooms 240–350F. Open mid May–mid Oct.

Chabrol, rue Gambetta (53) 05.70.15: sorry, another pricey hotel in lovely riverside position. Jean-Claude Charbonnel deserves his Michelin star. Superb salmon pâté; succulent chicken in truffled sauce. Meals 80–200F. Rooms 140–180F. Check winter closing.

At Bourdeilles (10km on D78) – Griffons (53) 05.75.61: 16th-century house by river bridge, converted by patronne-chef Denise Deborde. Good cooking. Menu 75–150F; rooms 185F. Open 1 April–1 Oct.

Delightful old town beside river Dronne in Périgord, rich in old buildings, including riverside houses with flowered balconies and vines, and riverside gardens with willows. You enter by a 16th-century elbow bridge leading to the old abbey church, with 12th-century belfry and a fountain garden with a bust of the scandalous 16th-century abbot, diplomat and witty cynical chronicler of court life known as 'Brantôme' (Pierre de Bourdeilles).

Superb riverside strolls. Monastery buildings now town hall, schools and Bernard Desmoulin museum which includes works by this artist, painted, they say, when under the influence of a medium. He died in 1914.

7km on D18: Bourdeilles Castle, over which the Plantagenets and French squabbled for years; set spectacularly up a cliff side above the river, village and medieval mill. Superb! Brantôme's family built a Renaissance palace on to it.

D939
Périgueux
(27km)

Restaurants in Périgueux inevitably charge a lot for pâté de foie gras and truffles – most costly items. Truffles appear in many dishes, too. To really *taste* them, you must try them 'sous les cendres', moistened with spirits, wrapped in sheet of fat bacon and cooked in ashes. But why stuffed goose neck should be so dear is a mystery. It's a sort of sausage. An old peasant proverb says: 'A neck of goose and a bottle of wine and you can ask a friend to a banquet.' Another poor man's dish taken over by gourmets!

Léon, cours Tourny (53) 53.41.93: Henri Raynaud, truly great chef, has had his restaurant's austere front brightened and added a few 'nouvelles' dishes with light sauces – great concession. I shall stick to his superb Perigordian sauces. All great from simple 40F menu to regional 48F and gastronomic 110F. Try all Perigordian dishes; also salmon-trout with chives, duck stuffed with cèpes, snails in garlic sauce. Excellent wines and service. Shut Monday.

Domino, pl. Francheville (53) 08.25.80: old style, warm charm, pretty garden with restaurant. Genuine local dishes. Excellent wine cave. Menu 55–180F. Rooms 80–250F.

The white domes of the cathedral, as you enter the capital of Perigordian food, also promise an architectural feast; alas, many old buildings have been destroyed. The curious 12th-century cathedral, St Front, owes its flamboyance to the 19th-century architect Abbadie (called The Wrecker) who, when 'restoring', added seventeen turrets. Medieval houses can be seen from Barris bridge and in the old town.

Périgueux changed sides between France and England twice during 100 Years' War, finally opting for France. Pleasant drive to two ancient abbey churches, Chancelade and Marlande in Feytaud Forest (back along D939, D710 for very short distance; right on D1; then D2).

Périgueux
continued

Du Périgord, rue Victor Hugo (53) 53.33.63: 2-star Logis with pleasant rooms, garden with tables; good value meals; try beef fillet in Périgueux sauce. Menu 42–95F; rooms 60–140F. Much praise from readers.

Hostellerie du Moulin et du Château de Rognac (8km by D5 near Bassilac) (53) 54.40.78: Logis in unusual turreted 16th-century house; local cooking and wines; try duck confit, truffled omelette; menu 60–145F; rooms 115–190F. Shut 1 Nov.–1 April.

N89 Le Lardin-St Lazare (46km) Terrasson (4km)

Hotel Sautet, Lardin (53) 50.07.22: friendly, simple, food recommended by locals; nice garden. Try fillet of goose and duck; menu 40–125F. Rooms 80–175F.

18th-century Palladian Château Rastignac, on right of road, said to have inspired Washington's White House. Burned down by Nazis, 1944, partly restored.

Le Lardin is small town in lovely valley of river Vézère. It produces paper which sometimes produces a pungent smell. Terrasson is a lovely old town built in tiers up river bank, with 12th-century bridge. Deals in walnuts from nearby farms, and truffles.

N89 Larche (12km)

Hotel Boussier (55) 85.30.11: family-run (3rd generation) village inn used by locals; surprising swimming pool in garden; old simple rooms; always known for good food but a few recent criticisms of cheaper menu and 'brusque service'. Too busy, perhaps?

Tiny roads southward towards Souillac almost deserted; woods, hamlets, farms; delightful silent land; expect to get lost.

I have had good meals, especially cèpes omelette, crayfish (écrivisses) and duck confit. Menu 50–110F. Rooms 120–160F. Open 1 April–1 Oct.

N89 Brive la Gaillarde (11km)

La Crémaillère, ave Paris, (55) 74.32.47: Charles Raynal offers a super menu 'Carroir' (of the area) at 65F; try stuffed goose neck; goose liver; salads with walnut oil (delightful); outstanding desserts. Long wine list. Menu 55–90F. Rooms 90–160F. Shut 24 Aug.–8 Sept. Mon; Sun. evening off-season.

Chapon Fin, pl. Tassigny (55) 74.23.40: nice comfortable hotel with gastronomic dishes and cheaper meals. Menu 45–90F. Rooms 90–130F. Open all year.

Pleasant, friendly if unexciting town. Hôtel de Labenche is a fine Renaissance mansion; now a library, but you can see it from the courtyard.

D38 Collonges (21km)

Relais St Jacques de Compostelle (55) 25.41.02: most attractive; good variety of dishes and prices. Menu 34–120F; rooms 61–116F.

Le Prieuré (55) 25.41.00: charming flower-decked house; willing service; inevitably full in season; excellent cooking, genuine ingredients; try anything – fine pâté; omelettes with cèpes or truffles; confit d'oie (conserved goose); guinea fowl flambé; coq au vin. Menu 50–115F; rooms 45–72F.

Reached through wooded hills and valleys, set among walnuts and vines, this charming old city is called La Rouge for the dark red stone of its mansions, old houses and 12th-century fortified church, which has a gun-room from the 100 Years' War. Fortified, too, is the elegant house of the Viscounts of Turenne-Castel de Vassinhae. Leave your car at former railway station and walk. Fine old houses. Can get crowded high-season.

D38 through
Meyssac, D940
to Bretenoux,
then D14, D43
to Castelnau
(30km)

Hotel Bureau, Biars-su-Cère, Bretenoux station (65) 38.43.54: pleasant Relais in same family 50 years. Menu at 38F good value; cheap wine; lovely trout in wine. Don't expect wonders at these prices – a few readers do! Most love it. Rooms 50–65F. Chance to recoup if you have overspent on Perigordian feasts.

Meyssac is a nice market-town in red clay, surrounded by rolling country of fruit, vineyards, walnuts and poplars. Old wooden houses and towers. Castelnau Castle is three miles round – a formidable red-stone fortress standing guard over the Cère and Dordogne rivers, with lovely views of both from ramparts. Built in the 11th century, extended in the 100 Years' War, it was restored from 1896 to 1932. Once it had a garrison of 1500 men and 100 horses. Its rent was then one egg per year, carried in pomp by four oxen to the Viscount of Turenne. Lovely Romanesque windows and tapestries of Aubusson and Beauvais (shut Tuesdays).

D14 over river
Bavé, left on
D30 to D673
past Château
Montal to St
Céré (10km)

Hotel de Paris et du Coq Arlequin, boulevard Dr Roux (65) 38.02.13: delightful; in Bizat family 100 years. Charming furnishings; Lurçat tapestry of Coq Arlequin in dining room; restaurant named after one. Good value. Menu 58–140F; rooms with breakfast 150–250F. Shut Jan., Feb.

Parc Hotel (65) 38.17.29: pretty gardens; bedrooms improved; friendly; but since change of ownership many readers give no praise for cooking. Menu 45–160F; rooms 66–165F. Shut December.

Château Montal is a 'phoenix' castle. Jeanne de Balsac built it in 1534 for a son who was away at the wars, hiring the greatest artists and builders. Only his body returned, and his grief-stricken mother had her window blocked up. In 1879 an asset stripper auctioned its treasures and sold much of its stone for building in Paris. In 1908 a new owner had it repaired and bought back the treasures from museums and collections at ransom prices. One stone doorway was missing, so Rodin, the great sculptor, made a new one.

St Céré is splendid – a smiling little town with the river Bavé running through its streets and flower-decked riverside houses. St Laurent tower, overlooking the town from a steep hill, was the home until he died recently of Jean Lurçat, the great tapestry and ceramic artist. Many of his works are displayed permanently in St Céré 'casino', around a big pleasant bar.

D673 past Grotte de Presque to Padirac (14km)

Grotte de Presque is made up of caves pillared with slim and thick stalagmites 10m (30ft) high, and of strangely varying shapes. Gouffre de Padirac is a chasm made, it is said, by the heel of the devil who taunted St Martin to jump it. He did it – all 325 feet of it – on a mule, a feat worthy of Harvey Smith. A refuge shelter during the 100 Years' War and the Huguenot wars, it was neglected until 1890. By lift and stairs, you descend 110m (338ft) to a chamber, then walk to an underground river. Here you board flat-bottomed boats for an unreal trip over strangely translucent waters for half a mile to visit more chambers on foot.

D673 Alvignac les Eaux (5km)

Hotel Palladium (65) 33.60.23: restful, attractive; excellently run by vhe charming Mme Vayssouze; garden swimming pool; views; modern bedrooms

Pleasant, quiet village, with nearby spa waters prescribed for disorders of the liver and digestion. Good centre for seeing Rocamadour, Padirac and other crowded sites.

Alvignac les Eaux *continued*

excellent; some old ones small. I love it. Cooking is very good – light but rich. Subtle use of truffles, cèpes, confit of goose. Menu 55–120F. Rooms 150–180F. Open 1 May–1 Oct.

Nouvel Hotel (65) 33.60.30: Modern, clean, fair value; menu 31–115F; rooms 53–100F. Shut Jan., Feb.

D673 Rocamadour (10km)

Most restaurants are tourist-bait. I would stay at Alvignac – Ste Marie Hotel (65) 33.63.07: rococo décor; comfortable; good bourgeoise cuisine, generous portions. Menu 45–120F; rooms 100–180F. Shut 15 Oct.–Palm Sunday.

Hostellerie Bellevue, l'Hospitalet (65) 33.62.10: comfortable; fine views of Rocamadour; gastronomic regional dishes, local wines. Menu 50–180F; rooms 65–175F. Shut Jan.

At Gramat, 11km N140 – Lion d'Or, pl. Republique (65) 38.73.18: fine country inn; enthusiastic patron-chef René Mommejac scours countryside for best ingredients for genuine Quercy cooking, using old recipes. Try a starter of crayfish with green beans and duck liver and progress from there! Superb. Menu 50–180F; rooms 140–185F. Shut Dec., Jan.

This tourist cliché of a medieval city clamped on a 150m (500ft) rock face is magnificent despite too many tourists and shops. View it first from the road terrace at l'Hospitalet above, preferably at night or in the morning sun. You will never forget it. From the castle at the top, the town works its way down through a maze of old houses, towers, rocks and oratories to a road still high above a river valley. It was founded near the top by St Amadour, a recluse, and pilgrims used to climb the 216 steps to the ecclesiastical city on their knees and in chains. Today very few kneel at every step. It would be unwise even to *walk* up the steps after a typical meal in one of the restaurants which abound around here. Chapelle Miraculeuse is where the hermit is said to have hollowed an oratory out of the rock.

D32 D677
Labastide
Murat (24km)

They changed its name in honour of Jean Murat, the general whom Napoleon made King of Naples after displays of fanatical bravery on battlefields – and after he married Napoleon's sister Caroline. After Bourbons returned to Naples in 1815, he tried to recapture 'his' kingdom, was captured and shot. His modest birthplace is now a museum. The inn is named after him too.

D677, N20 then local roads into town to see Lot Valley. Cahors (35km)

Almost gourmand country, with temptation to overeat. The vineyards produce a good strong red Cahors wine (alas, recently discovered by Parisians) and Blanc de Lot.

La Taverne, rue J-B-Delpech (65) 35.28.66: Pierre Escorbiac has gone! Oh, dear! Another of the old school of superb sauces and man-size meals has left us. But good news! Spies tell me that young Patrick Lannes, Paul Bocuse chef, has altered neither the eccentric décor, the splendid old-fashioned classic cuisine nor the splendidly filled wine cellar. He has added his own plats du marché of fresh seasonal dishes. I'll be there soon! Menu 50–150F. Shut November.

A lovely old town in a superb position in and around a horseshoe of the river Lot, with vine-covered hills behind. The fortified medieval bridge with three slim towers, Valentré, is one of the most beautiful in the world. Legend claims that the Devil himself helped to finish it on time, then was tricked out of payment. St Etienne's Cathedral, also fortified, founded 1119 and altered until 1500, has medieval paintings and a supremely lovely medieval door. The town is rich in old buildings and surrounding country reminds me of the Dordogne twenty-five years ago before the main stream of travellers found it. Magnificent view of town and river from Mont St-Cyr, but reached on foot by steep path from near Louis-Philippe Bridge (1½hrs).

Cahors
continued

Rest. Le Fénelon, pl. Emilion-Imbert (65) 35.32.38: good value; good 40F meal, excellent 65F; real Quercy 108F menu. Happy atmosphere. 1900 décor. Wines reasonable.

At Laroque des Arcs, 5km on D653 – Hostellerie Beau Rivage (65) 35.30.58: nice building beside Lot river; attractive; own stretch of fishing; naturally serves excellent trout. Also good crayfish, superb confit of duck with cèpes. Menu 40–120F. Rooms 100–130F. Hotel shut 2 Nov.–15 March.

N20 St Paul de Loubressac (20km)

Relais de la Madeleine (65) 31.98.08: excellent value; handsome Logis de France and Casserole Relais Routiers recommended for local dishes of Quercy; good value wines. Menu 35–140F; rooms 60–80F. Shut Sat. in winter.

N20 Montauban (40km)

Hostellerie les Coulandriers (4km on D958 towards Castelsarrasin) (63) 03.18.09: good discovery; nice house in lovely garden, roofed summer outdoor restaurant facing swimming pool; welcoming logfire in winter; Louis XIII-style restaurant. Every bedroom with bathroom, balcony; 8-acre park. Menu 80–180F; rooms 190–220F.

On a terrace above the river Tarn, this pink-brick market town is one of the most photogenic in France. At the end of the 14th-century bridge with seven arches is the 17th-century Bishop's Palace with many works of the 19th-century artist Ingres, a famous Paris teacher. He painted *Christ and the Doctors* when he was 82. In place Bourdelle alongside

Du Midi, rue Notre Dame (63) 63.17.23: behind banal exterior, a comfortable, well-run hotel; good cooking, excellent cassoulet with goose; menu 50–80F; rooms 60–180F.

you can taste local fruit free in season. The palace ground floor has modern sculptures of Courdelle, follower of Rodin, and some by Rodin himself. Place Nationale is a fine square with 17th-century brick arcades.

D999 Gaillac, then N88 to Albi (73km)

Albi – Hostellerie St Antoine (63) 54.04.04: founded 1734, in same family two centuries; modernised, tasteful; some rooms open on garden; quiet. New dining room; old recipes such as gras-double (stew of ham, tripe, vegetables, garlic, herbs); excellent desserts; good wine choice (Gaillac fruity white, red Cahors). Menu 65–150F; rooms 150–320F.

La Reserve, Forvialane, just outside Albi on Route des Cordes (63) 60.79.79: country brother to St Antoine; gorgeous position in park beside Tarn river; swimming

Gaillac, wine town and working port on Tarn river, has fine old town of wood and brick houses and squares with fountains. Several wine caves open, including those of St Michel Abbey.

Albi is an impressive town, especially seen from its bridges; centre of the Albigensian sect, ruthlessly destroyed as heretics by the French kings. The red-brick St Cecilia's Cathedral is one of the best Gothic in France, and its 15th-century fresco *Last Judgment* is France's biggest picture. The walls

Albi
continued

pool; expensive, super bedrooms; I have not eaten here. 'Relais et Châteaux Hôtel de France'. Menu 65–190F; rooms 180–400F, demi-pension only in summer. Shut Dec.–Feb.

Le Vieil-Alby, rue Toulouse-Lautrec (63) 54.14.69: Logis recommended to me locally; I do not yet know it. Cassoulet with duck praised. Cheap house-wine; menu 35–120F; rooms 66–83F. Shut Sunday.

and windows are covered with Italian frescos. Archbishop's La Berlie palace alongside contains the most important collection of works of Toulouse-Lautrec, born here 1864.

N112 Castres
(42km)

La Caravelle, ave Roquecourbe (63) 59.27.72: belongs to Grand Hôtel; summer restaurant (15 June–15 Sept.); eat inside or in garden among massed flowers beside river. Patron/wine expert Jean Pierre Fabré sells splendid Gaillac (white, red, rosé). With it, try a classic cassoulet (Carcassonne recipe with preserved goose), salmon mousseline, superb local charcuterie or any classical dish beautifully cooked by chef Christian Lapeyrère, a great traditional sauce chef. Menu 50–90F. Shut Sat.

Grand Hôtel, rue Libération (63) 59.00.30: has comfortable rooms, all with bath, wc, 90–150F; same chef, cuisine and menu prices as Caravelle. Shut 15 Dec.–15 Jan.

Beautiful scenery. As a change from Lautrec's dancing girls, Castres museum specialises in the more sedate works of Goya, including four major pictures, and some by other Spanish painters, including Velasquez. Old balconied houses line the river Agout.

N112 D118
Carcassonne
(64km)

With Castelnaudry and Toulouse, this is the home of cassoulet, but do beware of cheap tourist versions made of white beans with a touch of fat pork and tough mutton; the real thing is beans with pork, mutton, sausage and confit of goose or duck, and costs money. It is really a winter dish for chilly hill villages – not for hot summer days. Most restaurants in Carcassonne's old city are for tourists whom they don't expect to see again. Choose carefully. Currently the best is: Le Sénéchal, rue Viollet-le-Duc (68) 25.00.15: genuine local cassoulet, with goose, but a wide choice under new owners, the Tapie family – already well known as restaurateurs. As much free house-wine as you like! Menu 60–130F.

Auberge du Pont-Levis, at city gates (68) 25.55.23: renowned restaurant with good value 'snack' grill La Brocherie on ground floor; gastronomic restaurant with fine views of city towers on first floor. Another genuine cassoulet, good duck dishes and tasty pigeon. Best local wines, including Fitou. Menu 100–150F. Shut two weeks in June.

This medieval city, rebuilt in 1844 and called a fake by purists, is superbly done and makes the Middle Ages live again; despite too many tourist shops and cafés, you expect a pikeman lurking round every corner. Original fortified city withstood a five-year siege by Charlemagne.

Carcassonne
continued

Logis de Trençavel, ave Gen-Leclerc on N113, (68) 25.19.53: 3-star Logis de France serving one of the best cassoulet I have tasted; try also trout soufflé, crayfish dishes, and lotte (often a dull fish) in thick crayfish sauce. Some carping by snobbier French guides does not alter my high opinion of young patron-chef Rodriguez's cooking. Fitou too. Menu 80–105F; rooms 80–155F. Shut Weds. off-season.

From Carcassonne N610, D11 to Béziers (78km)

Compagnie du Midi, boulevard Verdun (67) 28.78.59: comfortable hotel with local supporters; known for its special fish soup; try also chicken with crayfish sauce and (far from home!) quail à la Normande. Menu 66F; rooms 120–170F.

Or N113 to Narbonne (56km)

Lion d'Or, ave Pierre Semard (68) 32.06.92: family-run, friendly, simple Logis where Michel Bonnet makes every effort to look after British guests and his chef strives for top quality in local and regional dishes. Local wines, too – Corbières, Minervois, La Clape. Menu 35–65F; rooms 70–140F.

Mapotel du Languedoc,
boulevard Gambetta (68)
65.14.74: pleasant old hotel,
well renovated; wide range
of dishes from tripes à la
mode de Caen to Valencian
paella, and Languedoc
cassoulet; honey soufflé;
menu 55–120F; rooms 75–
200F. Shut Jan.

Or N118 to
Limoux, D118,
D117 to
Perpignan
(120km)

Route 2
Le Havre to
Aix en Provence

You can taste the freshwater fish of the Loire on this route, then compare it with the salmon of the river Allier, trout and crayfish of the Auvergne, cooked in good local butter. They are especially luscious around Vichy. Pork is delicately excellent, too, even the salted belly used in potée auvergnate (with cabbage, potatoes and root vegetables). Vegetables are good, especially carrots. Ham is almost as good as in Ardennes, and there is a big variety of sausages large and small; also fungi from cèpes to morilles. Good cheeses are Bleu d'Auvergne, hard tasty Cantal and strong fourme d'Ambert. Vichy's Milliard is excellent (black-cherry tart made with batter).

The Ardèche has beautiful river fish, good charcuterie and old-fashioned mutton. You can still taste beautifully cooked, genuine hare in the Auvergne, and coq au vin nearly to Burgundy standard.

Vaucluse cooking is nearer to true Provençal – oil, lots of garlic, including aïoli (mayonnaise rich in garlic which is slapped over everything from veg to fish – and the name is used for village feasts – where pots of it stand on the table and barrels of wine surround you). You can have bourride – lighter, subtler bouillabaisse, with the liquid served as soup, then the fish with aïoli.

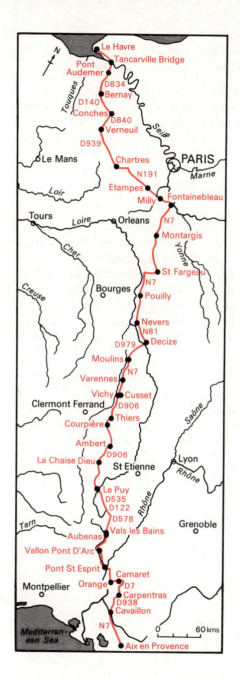

Le Havre
Tancarville Bridge
Pont
Audemer
Touques
D834
Bernay
D140
Conches
D840
Verneuil
D939
Le Mans
Chartres
Seine
PARIS
N191
Marne
Etampes
Milly
Fontainebleau
Tours
Loir
Loire
Orleans
N7
Montargis
Cher
Yonne
St Fargeau
Creuse
Bourges
N7
Pouilly
Nevers
N81
D979
Decize
Moulins
N7
Varennes
Vichy
Cusset
Clermont Ferrand
D906
Thiers
Courpière
Saône
Ambert
D906
La Chaise Dieu
St Etienne
Lyon
Rhône
Le Puy
D535
D122
D578
Tarn
Aubenas
Vals les Bains
Rhône
Grenoble
Vallon Pont D'Arc
Pont St Esprit
Camaret
Orange
D7
Montpellier
Carpentras
D938
Cavaillon
Mediterran-
ean Sea
N7
0   60 kms
Aix en Provence

In Provence you are truly in oil, garlic, fish and tomato country, with some magnificent dishes.

Wines of the Loire and Allier include Pouilly Fumé, smoky, fashionable and now pricey. Sancerre, growing popular so rising in price, and cheaper Sauvignons which the British are taking up. Little-known Gigondas red is almost as nice as Châteauneuf du Pape, but sharper, as the French like their wine. Baume de Venise nearby has a Muscat dessert wine – *really* sweet.

A south of Paris route with a chance to see Chartres and Fontainebleau; a little like the old N7 route of pre-motorway days, but taking in a little of the spectacularly rugged Auvergne countryside, the river Allier valley, the superbly lovely hills around Vichy and the valley of the Ardèche river which runs parallel to the Rhône. This canoeing river runs through steep ravines and past little beaches and is excellent for fishing.

Try to find time for the diversion from Orange into the Vaucluse to Gigondas – an area of lovely scenery and little wine villages where they see few tourists. A few connoisseurs of 'unknown France' spend their holidays here. Leave time to see Orange, a delightful town.

From other ports you can join the route at Bernay, Conches-en-Ouche or even at Chartres.

Route 2
Le Havre to
Aix en Provence

Badly off for hotels and not in the top league for meals. Cheap, quick, filling meals are available from the line of restaurants on Quai Southampton opposite Townsend booking office.

Monaco, rue de Paris (35) 42.21.01: Max Lucas, once mâitre d'hôtel on the liner *France*, and his young Breton chef offer an enormous choice with wide price-range. Near dock gates; very popular. Try jugged duck in Bouzy wine, cassoulet of lobster Neuburg, kidneys in Calvados; usually has superb oysters; Norman apple soufflé. Menu 55–150F; rooms 85–145F. Shut late Feb.; early Sept.

Mon Auberge, rue Gen-Sarrail (35) 42.44.36: Odette Mailly cooks superbly but has only six tables, so book ahead. Evenings only; menu 52F; à la carte dishes include turbot with wonderful Dieppoise sauce of cream, shrimps, mussels and wine, super mussels in a court-bouillon, excellent terrines of rabbit and duck, and apple tart, Normandy style. Shut Sun.; early August.

A modern town with 'son of Corbusier' architecture, planned after terrible wartime destruction. Avenue Foch is like a modern version of Champs-Élysées, with many shops at expensive Paris level. Auguste Perrett's place de l'Hôtel de Ville is one of Europe's largest squares. Arcaded rue de Paris, leading from the square towards the port, is useful for window shopping in rain or wind; windows of elegant clothes, tempting food. The huge concrete Church of St Joseph has an eight-sided belfry 116m (348ft) high, and the interior has an awesome lantern tower and remarkable inside lighting effects by coloured glass set in the walls; a most interesting building.

The Musée des Beaux-Arts, in glass and steel, facing the sea, has splendid light to show off Impressionist paintings, including seventy by Dufy, others by Sisley, Boudin and Pissarro.

Le Havre
continued

La Chaumette, rue Racine (35) 43.66.80: small, popular, expensive, thatched roof and fake beams amid Le Havre's concrete and glass; but very good for fish and duck; dishes according to what is fresh in the market and 'the knowledge and inspiration of the chef-patronne Christine Frechet. You must book; menu 120F. Shut Sat., Sun. and late August.

La Petite Auberge, rue St Adresse (35) 46.27.32: used by locals; good fish; good value; menu 58–75F; shut Mon.; August.

At St Adresse, suburb NE – Beausejour, pl. Clemenceau (35) 46.19.69: right beside sea, with panoramic views; many superb fish dishes; live lobsters; menu 70–145F; wines 40–800F.

D982 to Tancarville bridge (toll) (29km) D810 Pont Audemer (19km)

Three superb restaurants here – Auberge du Vieux Puits, Le Petit Coq and La Frégate. All very dear.

La Frégate, rue La Seule (32) 41.12.03: cheapest of the three. Lovely crab soup and moules à la creme; menu 85F plus carte; wines 45–350F. Shut August; Sun. evening; Monday.

At Campigny (6km on D29) – Le Petit Coq aux Champs (32) 41.04.19: now that the menu at Auberge du Vieux Puits costs 175F, I have switched my expensive celebrations to

Little port on several branches of river Risle. One of my favourite hideaways for 43 years; many of its old wood and brick riverside houses blessedly survived war damage; so did the streets and courtyards off rue de la République, and St Ouen Church, started in the 11th century. Its superb Renaisssance stained glass by no means clashes with modern windows by Max Ingrand, with their unusual use of colour. The 17th-century Auberge du Vieux Puits, once my favourite,

this little Cock, where you can get away with 135F. A Relais de France. Charming, thatched, elegant rusticity; log fires. Wonderful welcome from the Pommier family. Dinner, bed and breakfast for two people, 750–880F. Definitely for anniversaries.

Au Rendez-vous des Chauffeurs, rue Notre Dame (32) 41.04.36: where I usually eat. Next door to Vieux Puits – a Relais Routiers. Splendid value menu at 28–45F. Simple, cheap rooms.

now a bit film-set inside, with Michelin rosette and prices beyond me. Food as good as ever.

D810, D834
Bernay (33km)

See **Route 1**.

D140 Conches-en-Ouche (34km)

La Grand'mare, ave Croix de Fer (32) 30.23.30: charming Logis with 10 pleasant rooms; opposite a small lake; good value; patron-chef Jean Dubois cooks very well; try mussels in cream sauce, salmon, apple and Calvados soufflé, crab soup; menu 55–150F. Rooms 60–95F. Shut Tuesday.

La Toque Blanche, place Carnot (32) 30.01.54: fun restaurant with Norman cooking; old Norman building with staff dressed in old Norman costume. Menu 60–89F.

You pass on the way Château de Beaumesnil, a 17th-century house, reflected in its moat, in a classical French park; farm maintained since 1640; ponds; labyrinth of yews made from foundations of medieval dungeons. Curious line of owners, from Harcourt family to Lord Willoughby (a present from Henry V), Marquis of Nonant, Grand Duke Dimitri of Russia and Jean de Furstenberg. A gorgeous house.

D840 Verneuil-sur-Avre (22km)

Hostellerie du Clos, rue de la Ferté-Vidame (32) 32.21.81: small turreted manor house in gorgeous garden; menu 95F. Good dishes include a soufflé glacé au Calvados; rooms 200–280F. Relais de France. Shut Mondays and 15 Dec.–20 Jan.

Flamboyant tower of La Madeleine Church as fine as Butter Tower of Rouen, and similarly paid for by rich gourmands who in return could eat butter during Lent. One tax our Chancellors have so far missed. Fine old houses nearby.

D939 Chartres (56km)

A big tourist centre, so restaurants, especially round the cathedral, tend to be competitive in price, with mediocre cooking. These I found to be good value:

Buisson Ardent, rue Lait (37) 34.04.66: shut, alas, Wed., Sunday evenings and August. Good 45F menu; excellent 68F menu; imaginative dishes; home-smoked beef and salmon; frogs'-leg soup, lettuce soufflé, cèpes glacés as a dessert (glazed fungi) – as well as a fine rabbit stew and a grilled contre-fillet of beef.

L'Ecu, rue Grand-Faubourg (37) 21.34.59: country-style, with pleasant, friendly service. Try smoked pork; pheasant; good cheeses; truffled boudin sausage. Menu 46–70F; rooms 52–100F. Shut Sun. evenings, Mon.

Auberge St Maurice, rue St Maurice (37) 21.13.89: 'Casserole' Relais Routiers, serving well-cooked local dishes; big portions at low prices. Shut Sundays. Pretty house in old quarter.

The city on the river Eure is dominated by its cathedral on a hill; it is the best-proportioned and one of the most impressive churches in the world; consecrated in 1260, it is rather dark and sombre inside, but has unsurpassable medieval stained-glass windows. The terrace has good views over the river, and the Bishop's Palace here is now a museum with Flemish tapestries and paintings. The original cathedral was burned down in 1194, and to build the new one everyone from paupers to princes gave their money and labour; monks, peasants and ladies of the manor worked together on the scaffolding. Take time to see Renaissance houses around cathedral and wander down to river to see old bridges and houses. A charming town.

N10, N191 Étampes (58km)

This is 80km (50 miles) from Paris; the restaurants rely heavily on Parisians who drive out and locals who work in Paris, hence some have Parisian prices and summer closures.

In very attractive position on Chalouette river, with riverside walks; many lovely old buildings. In 14th century was seat of ruling regent, Abbé de St Denis, while Louis VII was fighting a Crusade, and it rivalled Paris.

Étampes
continued

L'Europe (À l'Escargot), rue St Jacques, 494.02.96: good value but inconvenient closing; known for snails and lamb. Menu 35–40F. Shut Weds.; rooms 55–90F. Shut 25 June–25 July; 15 Sept.–6 Oct.

At Chalo-St-Mars (7km on D21) – Les Alouettes, 495.40.20: country auberge, attractive décor, imaginative dishes – when open! Menu 70F but many dishes carry supplements; try local duck with turnips. Shut Weds., Thurs.; 10 Aug.–10 Sept.

Lovely drive in Chalouette valley through very pleasant villages – Chalo-St-Mars, Moulinex, Chalou (D21, D160). At Bierville (D49) is l'Epi d'Or, France's first youth hostel (opened 1929).

D410 Milly
(26km)

Old town on edge of Fontainebleau forest. Its fine buildings include market halls made entirely of oak. Chapel of St Blaise-des-Simples (12th-century) restored in 1958. Tomb of Jean Cocteau (1889–1963), one of the greatest writers, artists and, above all, playwrights of all time. He decorated the chapel in 1959 with lovely drawings of the Crown of Thorns and the Resurrection.

5km north is Château de Courances, magnificent 17th-century building in a park laid out by Le Nôtre, who also laid out Versailles and Fontainebleau gardens; it is packed with moats, ornamental lakes, waterfalls and fish ponds; you can visit it on Saturdays, Sundays and public holidays.

D409
Fontainebleau
(20km)

Most restaurants and hotels are dear and touristy. These are exceptions:

Ile de France, rue de France, 422.21.17: praised by France's leading food and travel writers and by many of my readers – but certainly *not* all. Food is Chinese by a chef from Hong Kong but, unlike here in Britain, loaded towards the French ('spicy imperial-style frogs'-legs' and trout in Chinese wine); one

Charming drive through the wild forest of pines, oaks and beeches; notices name some aged trees as if they were dogs, while others bear legends like STAG AND BOAR CROSSING. Rocks used as climbers' training grounds and torrents rushing between them. The château, not so impressive as Versailles, has as much historic importance and as much atmosphere. Louis VII began it, but the flamboyant Francis I made it into a palace, and brought in Italians Primatice and Rosso to decorate it. Benvenuto Cellini worked here for him and Francis bought the *Mona Lisa* to decorate a room – all for love of his mistress. Henry II kept his mistress Diane de Poitiers here too, and made her a special garden. When he died, his wife Catherine de' Medici took it over and sent Diane packing to Château de

Fontainebleau
continued

of France's greatest experts finds it good. Certainly not dear – menu 29.50 (with wine), 48, 68F. Louis XVI dining room, nice flower garden. Bedrooms fairly awful when Charles Glise arrived five years ago, now redecorated, all with own bath or shower and wc. Rooms 80–150F; family rooms (4–5 people) 200F.

Le Dauphin, rue Grande 422.27.04: large helpings, keen service, good straightforward cooking; Menu 45–70F. Shut Weds.; Feb.

Chaumont in the Loire. Louis XIV had the garden laid out, Napoleon I converted part of the château as his living quarters, imprisoned the Pope here, abdicated in the Red Room, and said farewell to his Old Guard in the courtyard. The guided tour shows you most things, but on most weekdays you can also see Napoleon and Josephine's rooms and those of Pope Pius VII. The château abounds in secretive nooks and crannies and back staircases, ideal for intrigue – or parties.

N7 Montargis
(51km)

Lyon, rue André-Coquillet (38) 85.30.39: much praise from readers for René Lefèvre's Logis. Old house attractively furnished; menu at 58F fair; 85F menu with½-bottle of good wine is better value; 90F menu excellent. Try turbot terrine, boeuf Bourguignon, matelote of river eels stewed in red wine, good trout; mouthwatering pear tart. Good choice cheapish wines; nice Sancerre. Rooms 50–160F. Shut Sun. evening, Monday.

Le Petit Relais, ave de Gaulle (38) 98.00.85: small, rustic interior, flowered terrace. Chef Robert Trancy, ex-Maxims in Paris, grills over huge log fire, many brochettes (try fruits de mer and lamb); good terrines; menu (lunch) 58–95F; evening à la carte,

Charming, little-known town of many streams; meeting of the Loing, Puiseaux and Vernisson waterways. Pleasant walks beside them.

N7 not quite so crowded these days. Motorways have taken much traffic.

reasonable prices; rooms 70–145F; shut Monday. Sited just off N7 on road opposite railway station.

D90 St Fargeau (51km)

Route beside canal and River Loing to this nice old country town with a rose-pink château, reconstructed in 1752; a pentagon with huge round towers and an elegant interior courtyard which can be visited (shut Tues. and Feb.); so can the beautiful park, with a large lake.

N65, N7 Pouilly sur Loire (59km)

Relais Fleurie et Rest. Le Coq Hardi, ave de la Tuilerie (86) 39.12.99: flower gardens, river view; excellent cooking by chef-patron Jean-Claude Astruc of duck; chicken in local wine; river fish (salmon; sandre – a local pike-perch, very delicate); try salmon à l'orange. Good value; menu 41, 69 (excellent), 90, 175F. Good wine list.

La Vieille Auberge (86) 39.17.98: a nice discovery; good value meals; sensible wine list. Menu 70–130F; shut Wednesday.

Home of Pouilly Fumé, the flinty dry white wine (not to be confused with Pouilly-Fuissé from Burgundy). Made from Sauvignon grapes, its recent popularity has made it rather dear. The litre-lappers' cheaper substitute, Pouilly-sur-Loire wine, is made from Chasselas, grown originally for Kings at Fontainebleau but not so fruity as Fumé. Do not judge this town from what you seen on N7; go down to the Loire and savour its river views (and wines) from Relais Fleurie (see restaurants).

N7 Nevers (40km)

Auberge Porte du Croux, ru P. du Croux (86) 57.12.71: very nice, pretty, quiet, terrace overlooking gardens with ancient city wall tower. Charming welcome. Fish direct from Atlantic coast – or from the Loire. Meal prices inevitably higher but

On the Loire where the river Nièvre joins it, Nevers is still famous for beautiful glass and enamelcraft introduced from Italy in 1575; it is also steeped in church history and has yet another much-visited cathedral, plus an interesting modern church looking as

Nevers
continued

still good value. Menu 84–
141F; rooms 89–95F. Shut
August.

Hostellerie La Folie, route des
Saulaies (86) 57.05.31:
modern, swimming pool;
Logis; very good value.
Menu 42–89F; rooms 80–
160F.

Hôtel Molière, rue Molière
(86) 57.29.26: no restaurant;
comfortable, good value
overnight stop; rooms 96–
139F.

solid as a Nazi West Wall but
interesting inside; it is called
St Bernadette du Banlay,
after St Bernadette of
Lourdes, whose uncorrupted
body is displayed macabrely
in a coffin of bronze and
glass in the Convent of St
Gildard in Nevers where she
died. I liked the convent story
of their 18th-century parrot
called Vert-Vert who was so
highly educated in Christian
doctrine that the monks of
Nantes asked to borrow him.
Alas, *en route*, the Loire
sailors taught him so much
blaspheming that the monks
sentenced him to solitary and
silence. He died of
indigestion, probably bottling
up his comments on the
Brethren of Nantes.

D13, D116
Decize (34km)

Built on an island in the Loire
river on a steep hill where
the Dukes of Nevers once
had their castle, it has a
lovely half-mile promenade
of massive plane trees. On
route, Chevenon Castle,
poised to control the valley.
Built in 14th-century by a
commander of Charles V
regime; later centre for
looting and brigandry, typical
of the Wars of Religion in
France.

D979 Moulins
(33km)

7km N of Moulins on N7 at
Trevol – Relais d'Avrilly (70)
42.61.43: not to be
compared, of course, with
Moulins' Hôtel de Paris with
2 Michelin stars and prices to
fit, but very good value.

Not an exciting town but the
Gothic cathedral has a
remarkable triptych for
enthusiasts.

Ultra-modern 3-star Logis with heated swimming pool, very comfortable rooms, wood fires, dining room with big spit, opening onto a garden, super spit-roast beef on the bone, brochettes; try plateau St Antoine (charcuterie). Menu 52–90F. Rooms 195F.

N7 to Varennes
N493 to Cusset,
3km to Vichy
(57km)

Many luxe hotels and restaurants in this luxe resort. But some good cheaper ones.

Nièvre, ave Gramont (70) 31.82.77: real old-style 'corner café' with good value meals; known for real old coq au vin; menu 34, 45, 70F; nice regional wine lists; rooms 55–70F.

Marcotel et Restaurant Chateaubriand, across river bridge at Bellerive (70) 32.20.00: modern, very comfortable, views over river Allier; meals fine value, with splendid chef-patron who once cooked for the Aga Khan and guests; lovely rich sauces; try sole in vermouth; outstanding wine list, from local wines to grand crus, and 'almost all champagnes'. Menu 70–150F; rooms 149–223F.

At Abrest, on Thiers road – La Colombière (70) 98.69.15: lovely views and good cooking by chef-patron Michel Sabot; try veal chops in onion compôte; kidneys in raspberry vinegar; menu 55–100F; rooms 80–150F. Shut Jan.; Sunday evening, Monday in winter.

Vichy – elegant, fashionable and expensive spa with full season of shows in the Grand Casino, May–September, and many nightclubs and pricey restaurants where the well loaded undo the good done to them in the thermal establishment. Parc des Sources is lovely. Allier lake, 4km (2½miles) long, is a famous water-sport centre for sailing, water-skiing, canoeing, pedalos, trout fishing, a biggish sandy beach. The Romans discovered the advantages of the strongly alkaline waters of the Celestins spring. Madame de Sévigné, whose home is now the Hôtel Pavillon Sévigné, said in the 18th-century that 'the countryside alone would cure me', and I feel the same today; but Napoleon III, spa addict, started the real Vogue for Vichy in 1861. Lovely public gardens beside the river Allier.

D906 Thiers
(35km)

An attractive road to Thiers, which is beautifully sited above a gorge of the river Durolle, with super views; well worth spending time looking at the very beautiful and photogenic 15th-century timbered houses, especially in place du Pirou and surrounding streets; best views with orientation table, from Terrasse du Rempart; you can see the mountains of Dore and Dombes; or drive E along N89 past Bellevue to Martignet (5km), right on D102 back to Thiers. Several good views on your right (16km total).

D906 Courpière (16km)

Clef des Champs, 3km S on D906 53.01.83: I have not tried it, but recommended to me for good regional cooking in pleasant surroundings; menu 35F (little menu) – 75F. Shut Mon.; Feb.

At the entrance to a gorge of the river Durolle, it is loved by fishermen – also by gourmets for its raspberries and the dishes produced from them. Château de la Barge, on N106, is beautifully kept and, with huge round towers, makes a fine picture, but can be visited only on Tuesday afternoons – exterior and chapel. For Château d'Aulteribe you turn off N106 6km before Courpière and take D223, winding uphill; the château was rebuilt in the 19th century to replace a severely practical feudal castle once owned by Lafayette; contains beautiful Louis XV and Louis XVI furniture, Flanders tapestry, and portraits, by well-known artists, of Henry IV, Richelieu and the unfortunate Mademoiselle de Fontanges, mistress of Louis XIV; described as 'beautiful as an angel, stupid as a basket'; she died in childbirth when 20 'from wounds received on active service' as the bitchy Madame de Sévigné said.

D906 Ambert (39km)

Livradois, pl Livradois (73) 82.10.01: one of the cheapest restaurants starred by Michelin. Chef-patron Gaston Joyeux believes in old-fashioned cooking of fresh products of Auvergne countryside. Superb salmon poached in herby court-bouillon; ham crêpes; coq au vin; lake trout; Ambert blue cheese (magnificent); super Auvergne charcuterie; sound wines such as dry white St Pourcain; menu 70–100F; rooms 58–160F. Shut Monday; part Jan.–Feb.

D906 La Chaise Dieu (33km)

Au Tremblant (71) 00.01.85: one of six Logis here; comfortable; cheaper menus very good value. Try lake trout with almonds, coquelet au vin; good patisserie; menu 40, 60, 80F. Rooms 70–150F. Shut Jan., Feb.

Lion d'Or (71) 00.01.58: another Logis, opposite the abbey; friendly, good service. Traditional Auvergne cooking, well done. Try also mussel soup. Long, good wine list; house-wine 22F bottle; rooms 70–150F. Shut Jan., Feb.

A hilltop village; the 14th-century abbey is like an ecclesiastical art museum, with magnificent 16th-century tapestries of Bible scenes from Brussels and Arras and a huge mural *La Danse Macabre*. The abbey boasted some colourful abbots – two royal bastards: one, son of Henry II, an assassin, later killed in a duel; the other, son of Charles IX appointed when aged 13. Cardinal Rohan, 'not very strong in Devotion, strong in love of women', hid there. Richelieu 'added it to his beneficies' – i.e. stole it.

D906 N102 Le Puy (44km)

Hôtel du Cygne, boulevard Marechal-Fayolle (71) 09.32.36: in town centre; all bedrooms have private showers; pavement terrace and another overlooking the old town; well known for its tripe, but that is no reflection on its cuisine, which is local and good; try local grilled trout, trout soufflé, quail with myrtle. I like its wild mushrooms Provençale (most in France are those cultivated buttons these days and tend to be flavourless); menu 45–100F; rooms 65–180F. Shut Nov., Dec., Jan.

Au Grand Cerf, ave Charles-Dupuy (71) 09.05.51: Logis; excellent blanquette de veau; duck in orange; kidneys in Madeira; menu 45–82F; rooms 64F. Shut Monday; 15 Feb.–15 March.

At Bizac, 12km on N88 – Relais de la Diligence (Hôtel Bonnefoy) (71) 08.11.50: comfortable inn near Lake Bouchet. Good straightforward cooking: duck, pork, game; mountain sausage; menu 35–55F; housewine 21F and good Ventoux red 28F; rooms 50–100F. Shut Monday; Jan.

Hilly winding road through the extraordinary volcanic hills. Le Puy is an incredible place, surprising even the most sophisticated traveller; volcanic peaks stand within the town; on top of one, le Rocher St Michel, is an 11th-century Romanesque chapel, reached by steep steps and looking almost like a minaret. On the biggest peak, Rocher Corneille, 750m (2460ft) high, is a 112,000kg (110-ton) statue of Notre-Dame de France, made from 213 cannons captured from the Russians at Sebastopol in the Crimean War. The cathedral, a Romanesque building of the 12th-century, also has a slightly Oriental look and is impressive inside and out. I find the old abbey cloisters most attractive with tranquil arcades, lawns, and a glimpse of the cathedral. They make a monk's life seem quite alluring. Strange contrast in this town between its oddly attractive moon-like rocks and lush, green country around; a lacemakers' town for centuries, lace shops abound, its lace is exquisite – and very dear.

D535, D122, D578 Vals les Bains (92km)

Grand Hôtel des Bains (75) 37.42.13: pricey, but one of my favourite individualistic hotels; in a park with pool; restful, big old-fashioned bedrooms, nicely furnished, elegant, old-fashioned service; excellent cuisine,

A winding mountainous route with wonderful scenery, but harder driving than the main road through Aubenas. Vals is a charming town on the river Yolane near where it meets the Ardèche and surrounded by

plenty of choice; outstanding river fish; menu 70–110F; wines from 29F (Côtes du Rhône); rooms 140–226F. Shut Nov.–mid May.

L'Europe, rue Jean-Jaurès (75) 37.43.94: two poets were born in this old manor house, and the beauty of its dining room and Louis XVI lounge might inspire another. Albert Mazet, happy and friendly patron, 30 years a chef, cooks still with youthful enthusiasm – traditional cuisine with ingredients most carefully picked; he does his own shopping, accepts nothing but the best, relies on fresh, seasonal dishes. Try local trout in St Peray wine; hot chicken liver terrine with tomato sauce and cèpes; guinea fowl salmis in wine; local Comtasso pastry with layers of cream, custard and chestnut cream. Menu 60–85F; rooms 80–180F. Shut 1 Oct.–Easter.

lovely hills varying from deep woods to open pastures, sweeping down to rivers which flow through tiny villages and meadows to deep spectacular gorges. Suddenly rediscovered, Vals can get full in midsummer; a pretty place with gardens, swimming pools, a casino, curative baths and a 'bar' on the river promenade offering spa water, which is prescribed for 'sedating the stomach and stimulating the liver'; but note also, inscribed in the pavement of the main shopping street (rue Jean-Jaurès), this advice: A GOOD MEAL DESERVES A GOOD WINE.

The Ardèche is superb for fishing and canoeing, from open riverside beaches to spectacular steep gorges. A river best seen from a canoe – but for me that was 45 years ago!

Vals les Bains
continued

Vivarais, rue C.-Expilly (75) 37.42.63: improvements over two years; try trout in almonds; local charcuterie; chicken with crayfish sauce; confit of goose; good patisseries; menu 70–150F; diabetic menu; good middle-priced wine list. Rooms 180–250F. Shut 15 Nov.–31 Dec.

De Lyon et les Arcades, ave Farincourt (75) 37.43.70: pleasant house with arcaded dining terrace; one of nine Logis in Vals; menu 60–80F; patron's local wine 21F; rooms 135–175F. Shut 5 Oct.–1 April.

At Antraigues, village on D578 8km from Vals, try Lo Podello (75) 38.71.48: Hélène Baissade runs a gem of a restaurant; she is a painter, interior decorator and cook, and in a house beautifully decorated in local style, she serves local country dishes, well cooked, at reasonable prices; all fresh local produce, from soup to trout, stuffed lamb, vegetables to fruit tarts, her meals are a delight; four menus, from 40F (weekdays) to 150F. Shut June and Oct.; open Fri., Sat., Sun. in winter; all days 1 July–30 Sept.

N102 Aubenas (6km)

Col de l'Escrinet, St Etienne de Boulogne (75) 35.50.90: modern; panoramic views over Ardèche valley; park with pool; restaurant rated 3

Worth leaving N102 to see little town. Château owned since the 12th century by famous local families, but altered through the years, is

stars, hotel 2 stars; try kidneys in St Peray wine; duck with green peppers; freshwater crayfish tails; menu 60–150F; rooms 145–260F. Shut 15 Nov.–15 March.

now the town hall. Described by French experts as 'rude', meaning rugged; the courtyard is attractive; you can visit it throughout July and August, Saturdays and Sundays only in June. Aubenas makes delicious marrons glacés. Lovely views as you enter town, also from D259 and from Table d'Orientation 100m (330ft) from château.

N102, right on D579 to Vallon Pont D'Arc, follow D290 through Les Gorges d'Ardèche to St Martin then D901 to cross Rhône at Pont St Esprit (80km)

This is a hard driving road over the Corniche, and you can skip it by taking N102 and N86 parallel with the Rhône, but it has truly magnificent scenery, gorges and one splendid view after another. At Vogué, there is a 12th- to 17th-century castle you can visit. Bridge over the Rhône at Pont St Esprit called 'the beginning of Provence'.

D994, N7 Orange (24km)

Arène, pl des Langes (90) 34.10.95: praised by many readers; good value meals; regional cooking in old house with terrace; good fish, duck, game; menu 55–110F; wines from 26F include good Gigondas; rooms 135–170F. Shut Nov.

Orange is one of the most interesting, charming and surprising cities in southern France. It has a Roman theatre which is the best preserved in Europe and holds, 10,000 spectators. The city still has its imperial statue of Augustus Caesar,

Orange
continued

Le Forum, rue Mazeau (90) 34.01.09: price rise but still good value; menu 60F. Shut Sat. evening, Sun. except July, Aug.

La Pigraillet, colline St Eutrope (90) 34.44.25: a discovery but not cheap; very good cooking of very fresh produce; good cassoulet with goose; duck; superb desserts; pretty place, too. Menu 80–105F; terrace, garden (eat out in summer), pool and boules. Shut Mon.; 1 Nov.–31 March.

the third biggest triumphal arch in Europe, celebrating Julius Caesar's victories over the Gauls and the Greek-Massilian fleet. It gave its name to the Dutch Royal family and thus to the Irish Protestant political movement.

It has nothing to do with oranges; the name came from the Latin. William the Silent inherited the city in 1559 from the Chalon family and the Dutch prince tore down much of the Roman remains to fortify it, but used the theatre as part of the city wall. After the French got Orange back, under the Treaty of Utrecht, Louis XIV called the theatre 'the finest wall in my kingdom'. The Dutch kept the title 'Princes of Orange'. For a few years during the reign of William of Orange (William III), the town was actually united with England. And in the museum is a room full of paintings by Sir Frank Brangwyn.

The old houses and wooded squares and avenues of Orange are delightful; it is a place for sitting at a pavement café and watching life go slowly past. Though the N7 passes through the town, this does not matter so much since the motorway takes away much of the traffic.

D975 to
Camaret then
local roads to
Gigondas
(18km)

Gigondas – Les Florets (90)
65.85.01: my delightful inn
made from a remote
farmhouse is now better
known – so better book!
Delightful, copious meals;
Provençal dishes; try pieds
et paquets (tripe stuffed with
bacon and parsley in sauce
with boned trotters); coq au
vin; superb salmon mousse;
very good lamb. Vacqueyras
wine from own vineyard,
plus 18 Gigondas wines.
Rooms 133–144F. Menu 72–
94F. Shut Wed.; Jan., early
Feb.

Montmirail (90) 65.84.01:
elegant; garden; pool. Nice
salmon; menu 75–100F.
Restaurant shut Sun.
evening; Monday. Rooms
from 165F.

Beautiful wild country of the
Vaucluse, with tiny villages
and farms where you can
taste the Gigondas red wine.
Gigondas hilltop church and
village seem to belong to
another century. An eccentric
detour, but worth it for the
scenery and experience. If
you have time, drive up Mont
Ventoux from Vaison-la-
Romaine or Carpentras. One
of the greatest sights in
southern France. Huge
panorama from top (1912m/
6370ft). Lovely drive. Takes
most of a day (with time to
stop and stare). Baumes-de-
Venise, juft off N7, is typical
little Vaucluse town.

**D7 Carpentras
(17km)**

Hotel Safari, ave J.-H.Fabre (90) 63.35.35: modern Logis; pool; pleasant restaurant; rooms all with bath, wc; good traditional dishes; meals 55–85F; rooms 125–175F. Restaurant shut Sun. evening.

Carpentras is a market town with lively fruit stalls; a wine town, too, and known in France for its 'berlingots' a sweet like a caramel bulls' eye. Carpentras has a Roman triumphal arch, built, as in Orange, by retired Roman legionaries who settled in the town. It has also the oldest synagogue in France, last relic of a 16th-century ghetto.

**D938 L'Isle sur
la Sourge to
Cavaillon
(27km)**

At Velleron, just off D938 between Pernes and Sourge – Les Grands Pins (90) 38.11.81: modern; very comfortable; excellent meals for price; menu 45–95F; try Côtes du Ventoux wines; rooms 120–250F. Shut 1 Nov.–1 March.

Famous for melons, known well for other fruit and for vegetables, it has a splendid market every day in summer in place du Clos. A genuine little country town with the atmosphere of Provence. Behind the high altar of the old cathedral is a picture by Mignard of a bishop getting the better of the Coulobre, a man-eating monster who it was thought inhabited these parts in the Middle Ages.

**D938 Aix–en–
Provence
(49km)**

At Aix-en-Provence – Le Manoir, rue d'Entrecasteaux (42) 26.27.20: 18th-century mansion with historic 15th-century cloister; beautiful period furnishings; Relais de Silence. No restaurant. Rooms 169–290F.

La Bourguignonne, rue de la Masse (42) 27.52.46: used by knowledgeable locals; dishes of Burgundy, from salad to fondue; grills over wood fire. Menu 40–100F.

One of those tourist clichés which will not let you down; surrounded by lovely landscapes, it has fine old buildings, fountains, and majestic avenues flanked by cafés and restaurants; a university town and a spa; Cours Mirabeau, made in the 16th century, is one of the loveliest avenues in France, though named after the scandalous local count who joined the Revolution after a life of debts and debauchery and became a great orator.

At Celony, 3km on N7 – Mas d'Entremont (42) 23.45.32: converted farm; lovely; charming décor; lovely garden; pool; excellent cooking; try duck or duck liver terrine; menu 94F; wines rather pricey; rooms 200–220F (but nice); restaurant shut Sun. dinner, Monday lunch; all shut 1 Nov.–15 March

The Impressionist painter Cézanne was born, worked and died here, and you can visit his studio on avenue Cézanne. There is more to see in Aix than in most big cities, and it is a question of what to leave out unless you are staying; twenty-six Flemish tapestries in St Saveur Cathedral are interesting; they were made for Canterbury Cathedral in 1511 and bought by St Saveur in 1656. Kent missed something.

From Aix-en-Provence, the motorway and the old N7 road run just behind the coast from Ste Maxime and St Raphael through the whole Côte d'Azur to the Italian border and beyond.

Route 3
Dieppe to Modane
(for Italy)

A route to *enjoy*, with changing pleasant scenery, especially on the smaller roads, most interesting old towns, and a run down the top half of the Burgundy wine road. Finally, mountain scenery with lakes, streams and waterfalls. A dawdlers' route. Few Britons know the hilly forest in Normandy, the beeches of Lyons forest, and the well-groomed parklike forests of Compiègne and Laigue.

If you haven't been this way, you will find all sorts of hidden treasures.

Burgundy is a châteaux country almost as much as the Loire and Dordogne. And the Savoy is one of the loveliest areas of France.

A good start, too. Dieppe is friendliest of the ferry ports. But you can join easily enough from other ports, though you may miss Eawy forest. Beauvais is the obvious place to join the route, though I would prefer Forges-les-Eaux.

A gourmand will be tempted to stay in Dieppe – Norman cooking at its best, with rich cream and shellfish sauces, wonderful fresh fish, beautiful butter and meat from lush pastures, cream desserts and fresh fruit, all at reasonable prices.

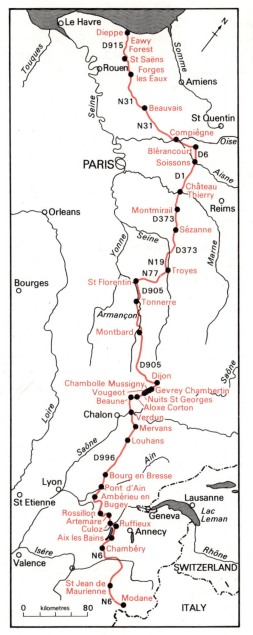

Le Havre
Dieppe
D915
Eawy
Forest
St Saëns
Rouen
Forges
les Eaux
Amiens
N31
Beauvais
St Quentin
N31
Compiègne
Oise
Blérancourt
D6
Soissons
Aisne
PARIS
D1
Château
Thierry
Reims
Orleans
Montmirail
D373
Sézanne
Seine
Yonne
D373
Marne
N19
N77
Troyes
Bourges
St Florentin
D905
Tonnerre
Armançon
Montbard
Saône
D905
Dijon
Chambolle Mussigny
Gevrey Chambertin
Vougeot
Nuits St Georges
Beaune
Aloxe Corton
Loire
Chalon
Verdun
Mervans
Saône
Louhans
D996
Ain
Lyon
Bourg en Bresse
Pont d'Ain
St Etienne
Ambérieu en
Bugey
Lausanne
Rossillon
Artemare
Geneva
Lac
Léman
Culoz
Ruffieux
Annecy
Aix les Bains
Chambéry
Rhône
N6
Valence
Isère
SWITZERLAND
St Jean de
Maurienne
N6
Modane
ITALY

Dieppe
PARIS
Modane

0   kilometres   80

As you leave the coast, you find poultry, especially guinea fowl and duck, game, and river fish, with plenty of good trout. Then more game in the Aisne forests until you reach Burgundy, with fine beef, charcuterie, crayfish, snails and frogs' legs. Dijon is the food capital of this route.

Around Bresse they produce what the French believe to be the best chickens in the world and cook them usually in cream and wine. Savoy's lakes and streams produce crayfish, salmon trout, trout and omble chevalier (small, slim salmon). Hams, salamis and sausages are plentiful in Savoy. Do try the soup of freshwater fish.

Normandy's Calvados (apple spirit) is used in cooking and as a digestive – you sink a glass quickly between courses to settle the stomach (called Trou Normand – the Norman hole). From Dijon south you have a glorious choice of Burgundy wines. Alas, even in Burgundy prices have risen painfully. The Japanese are blamed for bidding too high at auctions. But truth is that the whole world loves a Burgundy and there is not enough *genuine* wine to go round. We used to drink all sorts of things under labels marked 'Chablis', 'Pouilly', 'Beaujolais', 'Beaune' and 'Macon'. The French government seems to have stopped this nonsense.

Few Britons have tried Savoy wines. Whites, looking as pale as water, are mostly sparkling and refreshing. Seyssel wines are best known. Reds are not so good.

Chambéry produces a good white vermouth – light and dry.

Route 3
Dieppe to Modane
(for Italy)

Dieppe

Still has more good cheapish restaurants than anywhere in France. Some good value medium-priced, too.

Windsor, boulevard Verdun (seafront) (35) 84.15.23: Claude Lambert keeps up standards splendidly. Excellent Normande dishes (cooked in cream) and sole à la Dieppoise (cooked in white wine with mussels, crayfish, mushrooms and cream added); super scallop pâté; true Norman apple tart; cream gâteaux with Calvados. Sea views from dining room; menu 63–90F; rooms 75–170F. One of my favourites. Shut 15 Nov.–18 Dec.

L'Univers, boulevard Verdun (35) 84.12.55: Mme Tilquin's family have owned this comfortable hotel for generations and Jean Tilquin is a great chef. Every dish is succulent; try scallops, escalope Normande, tournedos crêpette, best cod (morue fraîche) I have tasted. Magnificent seafood platter. Outstanding Muscadet; extensive wine list; menu 70–100F; rooms 140–280F; shut most Dec. and Jan.

Step off the Sealink boat and you are truly in France, with bistros opposite, a fish market and pavement cafés for a plate of shrimps or moules marinières to a full meal. Grand'Rue is a pedestrian area, with shops selling a wide variety of things from expensive fashion shoes to cheap chickens and including a Prisunic chain store. There is a good wine shop and hardware store for kitchen equipment. On Saturday mornings, fishermen and farmers bring their produce to market – oysters, butter, farm pâté, and prawns are sold from stalls. The sea front has wide lawns, a beachside pool and a casino. Dieppe Castle, where Canadian soldiers in 1942 climbed the sheer cliff face, has a museum with navigation equipment, ivories and paintings, including works by the English Impressionist Sisley who worked gutting fish on this coast when starving.

Dieppe
continued

La Marine, arcade de la Poissonerie (35) 84.17.54: modern; younger locals use it for its excellent value; try matelote Marine (plate of fresh, local fish and shellfish); sole or turbot Dieppoise; creamed mussels; estouffade (beef in red wine and herbs); mirliton (apple and almond tart); good service; reasonable wines; menu 39, 55F (good value), 72F. Shut Tuesday evening, all Weds.

Marmite Dieppoise, rue St Jean (35) 84.24.26: a cliché in Dieppe – locals and tourist-regulars flock to simple-looking restaurant where fish is cooked superbly and chicken in cider very well. Willing service. That marmite Dieppoise (a Norman soup-stew of fish and shellfish, like Bouillabaisse) costs 70F or is in 110F gastronomic menu. 40, 63F menus not served Fri., Sat. evenings. Shut Sun. evening, Mon.; 20 June–4 July.

Normandy, rue Duquesne (35) 84.27.18: outstanding value in 'old Norman farmhouse' replica. Tables close; bustling service; candlelight in winter; huge choice even on cheapest menu; specialities chicken in cider, escalope à la Normande, shellfish omelette, apple and Calvados sorbet. Good cheap wines for 21F. Menu 36.50, 52, 76F. Shut Jan.

At Varangeville (8km) is a clifftop village church with superlative colourful modern window by Braque. His grave, designed by pupils in his style, is in the churchyard. Monet's painting of the church is now in the Barber Institute, Birmingham. He lived at Varangeville when he was too poor to afford canvasses. Parc Floralies, Varangeville, is a glorious garden. You can visit Ango Manor, strange 16th-century home of the corsair chief Jean Ango, a French 'Drake' who became Governor of Dieppe after destroying 300 Portuguese ships. Pourville has a museum of the 1942 Dieppe Raid, including tanks.

Du Port, quai Henri IV (35)
84.36.64: still popular with
locals, especially for fish
soup and turbot terrine with
langoustine sauce. Menu 53–
85F. Shut Thur.

Best place to find good,
really cheap meals is no
longer Quai Henri IV
(opposite Sealink boats) but
past fish market on Arcade
de la Poissonerie. Several old
bistro-style bar-restaurants
with menu outside from 25F.
Old-style names, too, like La
Victoire. A more modern,
ambitious restaurant here is:

La Moderne (35) 84.12.33:
two floors, modern décor;
good fish; also try guinea
fowl in cider. Menu 40, 56
(good value), 86F. Wines
from 22F. Shut Tues.
evening, Weds.

Useful, inexpensive overnight
hotel (with restaurant) is the
old Richmond, rue
Commandant-Fayolle (35)
84.22.33.

Pourville (4km) – Au Trou
Normande (35) 84.27.69:
Jean-Jacques Baton has left
my little old favourite; patron
Johnny Vaillant is in the
kitchen. Sounds like a pop-
star but I'm told he cooks
well and gives value.
Specialities: scallops in
season; brill barbue); menu
42–66F. Shut Sun. evening,
Mon.

Dieppe
continued

Puys (3km) – Domaine à Dumas (35) 84.15.70: inn called Auberge du Vieux Puits I knew as a boy has joined the upper classes. But Alexandre Dumas *did* live here. Menu 80–190F; menu of day 110F. Wines now *from* 40F; rooms 73–126F.

D915 to just before Torcy le Grand (34km); then D514 to St Helier, sharp left on to D97 into Eawy Forest, D12 on right, D118, D45 to St Saëns, N29 to Les Hayons crossroads, D915 Forges les Eaux (total about 60km)

Forges les Eaux – La Paix, rue de Neufchatel (35) 90.51.22: birth of a daughter, Cécile, in 1982 has not diverted Rémy Michel from his kitchen duties. Don't be put off by dull exterior. Excellent value; good old Norman farmhouse dishes like chicken in cider or 'vallé d'auge' (chicken in cream and Calvados – he cooks it as well as I do!); andouillette Normande (chitterling sausage); Norman apple tart. Menu 41, 50, 66, 84F; wines from 18F; rooms 51–84F. Shut Sun. evening, Mon.

Casino (at Casino) (35) 90.52.67: not my style but recommended to me for consistent value. Menu 65–90F. Don't gamble until you have paid for your meal.

A lovely drive through superb beech forest with deep valleys and lovely views. Road zigzags across Allée des Limousins, a long wide firebreak cut into forest. Some roads narrow and of dirt. Slow run.

Forges is a restful small spa; water was drunk regularly by Richelieu and Voltaire (who said it contained more vitriol than ink). Lovely park with sailing lake. Four rivers start here.

Cheese: it supplies more *fresh* cheese than any area in France. Not until 1850 did a local farmer's wife mix fresh cream and curds to produce demi-suisse.

On edge of Fôret de Lyons (beeches), 11th-century church. 11km on N30, then a local road, is Gerberoy, fortified hilltop town, almost abandoned in the 17th century until modern painter Le Sidaner (died 1939) and friends restored it.

N31 Beauvais (50km)

La Crémaillère, rue Guy-Patin, 445,03.13: local style with increasingly good regional cooking, mostly traditional and classic dishes; lovely ficelle Picarde (rolled pancake stuffed with cream and ham); very good desserts. Wines from 22F. Menu 55F. Shut Weds. except for reservations.

Palais, rue St Nicholas 445.12.58: comfortable bed and breakfast hotel near cathedral; no restaurant; rooms 85–145F.

Beauvais – Warluis (7km N1) – Des Alpes Franco-Suisses, 402.01.21: a break from Normande sauces and Calvados; looks and is run like a mountain hotel in Savoy. Small goats, deer and St Bernard dog in garden; cheese fondue, raclette, ice cream flambéed with William pear liqueur. Menu 32–78.50F; rooms 84–148F.

Superb old town regarded too often as half-day's excursion from Paris (76km). The cathedral, begun 1227, was never quite finished but is still magnificent in its new town setting. Highest Gothic choir in the world is awesome. Fine windows both old (14th to 16th centuries) and modern (include Max Ingrand and Braque). Magnificent Renaissance windows (and some modern) in St Etienne Church by Angrand le Prince. Do see place Jeanne Hachette, beautifully rebuilt after war damage and named after girl who rallied the French to victory by attacking the besieging Burgundy forces with an axe!

New National Tapestry Museum (by the cathedral) includes gorgeous tapestries from 15th century to today. The old museum was destroyed by bombing in 1940. Tapestry weaving started in Beauvais by order of Louis XIV. This art form revived in France in last 50 years, mainly through Jean Lurçat, who grew as an artist with Cocteau, Picasso, Matisse.

**N31
Compiègne
(57km)**

Hôtel de France et Rotisserie du Chat qui Tourne; rue E. Floquet, 440.02.74: the cat who turned the spit to roast a chicken belonged to a 'mountebank' who performed here in 1665. Now it turns by electricity. Charming old hotel; fine cooking, but not cheap; 'repas' 39.50F; menu 76.50F; gastronomic menu 165F; rooms 84–160F.

Le Picotin, place Hôtel de Ville, 440.04.06: traditional French cooking, pleasant; fair value; menu 40–70F. Shut Dec., Jan.

Flandre, quai République, 483.24.40: looks like a bank outside, a gentleman's club within; solid comfort; reliable, traditional cooking; menu 48–58F; rooms 80–150F.

In a huge forest 72km (45 miles) north of Paris, Compiègne is a town rich in art treasures. Here the kings of France always had a hunting hideout. Louis XV had a new castle built, rather severe but elegant. Louis XVI, when Dauphin, first received his fiancée here. It became a barracks, but Napoleon restored it as his castle home and Napoleon III and Empress Eugénie held impressive hunts and balls here. The rooms of Marie-Antoinette and the Napoleons retain their tapestries and furniture. Many Empire-period paintings including Boudins. Vivenel Museum has a vast collection of treasures spanning centuries, with superb Greek vases, and Musée de la Figurine Historique has 80,000 lead, wood and board soldiers. I love the Vehicle and Tourism Museum, with 150 vehicles from a Roman chariot to a Citroën chain-track car and including diligences (stage coaches), a post-chaise, superb sledges, a remarkable steam coach (1885) and early cars.

At Elincourt-Ste Marguerite (15km by N32 north and D142) – Château de Bellingese, 476.04.76: a bit pricey but what a delight! 16th-century Louis XVI château in pink with turrets and grey-green roof; set in big park with lake; one of the 'Châteaux Hôtels Indépendants' as opposed to 'Châteaux Hôtels de France'. Lovely furnishings; excellent chef; try baron of lamb with aromatic herbs; turbot in champagne. Wines 25–350F. Menu 80–160F; rooms 190–230F. Restaurant shut Sun. evening, Mon.

N31, D546 to Clairière de l'Armistice (5km)

In this lovely glade, Marshal Foch, commander of Allied Forces, received the German surrender in 1918 in a railway carriage. In 1940 Hitler insisted on receiving the French surrender here. Original carriage taken to Berlin and destroyed when Allies approached. So a replica coach stands in the glade, with genuine objects inside.

D81 Choisy au Bac, D130 through Laigue forest to D934, then right to Blérancourt (32km)

Blérancourt – Hostellerie Le Griffon (23) 52.60.11: charming, restful inn with pretty garden at castle gates; Parisians drive out on weekends to eat. Menu sensibly governed by market and seasons. Try salmon Pojarsky (super salmon 'fish cakes'); very good flamiche (leek, egg, butter and cream tart). Menu 60–110F; rooms 70–150F. Shut Sun. evening, Mon.

Lovely forest run, mostly beeches. Blérancourt is a quiet hideout of knowledgeable Parisians on relaxing weekends. It was the centre of terrible battles (1916–18). It was rebuilt by Ann Morgan, daughter of the US banker Pierpont Morgan, as a symbol of Franco-American friendship, and its castle dating from the 17th century houses a Franco-American museum mostly of

Blérancourt
continued

the Kaiser's war, including a superb T-Ford ambulance. Pretty gardens.

D6, N31
Soissons
(23km)

Rallye, boulevard Strasbourg (23) 53.00.47: small; useful for bed and breakfast; rooms 64–160F.

At Longpont (14km by D1, D175, D805) – Hôtel l'Abbaye (23) 96.02.44: near ancient abbey and Retz forest; recommended to me by French chef for beautiful meat grilled over wood; also hors d'oeuvres; menu 56–124F; rooms 90–140F.

Deeply involved in early French history from 486 AD when Clovis the Frank defeated the Romans. Rubens' superb *Adoration of the Shepherds* is in the 13th-century cathedral. He painted it in thanks for being nursed through a nasty illness here. Only the frontage remains of the original abbey where Thomas à Becket lived for nine years.

D1 (ex D37)
Château
Thierry (41km)

Turn left at Grand Rozoy and 12km along D2 at Fère-en-Tardois is Hostellerie du Château (23) 82.21.13: 2-star Michelin restaurant in a castle with a lovely park. Built 1206, and owned by Valois-Orleans family; passed to the Condé family; finally to Phillipe Egalité – Duke of Orleans (and friend of our Prince Regent, later George IV) who joined the French Revolution and knocked down part of the château as a gesture of 'equality'. He was still guillotined; present lovely building mostly 16th century. Very expensive but worth every franc. Superbly furnished. Magnificent cooking. Do try sea bass (bar) with truffled butter; fish salad; poêle de rognons (kidneys pot-roasted with vegetables); or duck breasts

The writer La Fontaine was born here in 1621 and the house, in a street now named after him, is a museum. Set on the Marne river, round a wooded hill in lovely country, the town has been involved in wars over centuries. The English took it in 1421, Joan of Arc recaptured it and entered

in vinegar of cassis (blackcurrant). Menu 160F and 240F. Rooms 260–325F. Perfect service. Shut 1 Jan.–1 March.

Hotel-restaurant St Eloi, ave de Soissons (23) 83.02.33: down to earth after the château; not much to look at but good cooking by chef-patron Raymond Barre and good value. Garden, terrace. Try trout in Marc (spirit) of champagne; chicken in champagne; true boeuf Bourguignon. 5 menus 40–100F; rooms 70F. Shut Weds.; 12–30 Sept., early Feb.

Ile de France, on N37 (23) 69.10.12: attractive hotel in green countryside with views over Marne valley. 5 menus 36–90F; good natural champagne (not fizzy) and red Bouzy. Rooms 70–200F.

through Porte Saint-Pierre which survives. In 1814 Napoleon defeated a force of Russians and Prussians just outside the town towards Montmirail. American units held it bravely and incredibly against a massive German attack in 1918, and hill 204 is part of American history. There is a momument and cemetery.

D1 Montmirail (24km)

Pleasant, old, with remains of ramparts, two very old churches and a château which you cannot visit.

D373 Sézanne (24km)

Hôtel de la France, rue Léon-Jolly (26) 80.52.52: continued accolades from delighted readers; it *looks* right, too; a gem. Try salmon terrine; sole or trout braised in Champagne; fine coq au vin; pigs trotters. Menu 58–68F. 400 different wines. Rooms 66–122F. Shut 15 Jan.–15 Feb.

Market town at meeting of three important roads, but still quite peaceful. Walks by ancient ramparts somewhat tortuous. Interesting Flamboyant Gothic church.

Westward is a pleasant drive through La Traconne forest (Château d'Esternay, Bricot-la-Ville-Colonne, Barbonne), about 37km.

Sézanne
continued

Croix d'Or, rue Notre-Dame (26) 80.61.10: another praised for value; pretty, creeper-clad; good traditional local dishes, well cooked by patron Jean-Claude Dufour; try mussels in Bouzy wine; crayfish – or peaches – in champagne. Good game and fish in season. Cheap and good wines. Menu 39–87F. Rooms (with bath, wc) 62–98F.

Relais Champenois et Lion d'Or, rue Notre-Dame (26) 80.58.03: handsome old building; pleasant country décor; good local dishes, especially creamed ham. Menu 38–55F. Rooms 62–92F. Shut Fri. and various weeks off-season (check).

D373, N19
Troyes (60km)

Le Bourgogne, rue de Gaulle (25) 43.06.03: still keeps our vote as best pricier restaurant around here, despite shutting August and Sundays, and counter-claims of M. Duquesnoy at his nearby Hostellerie de Pont-Sainte-Marie; cooking leans both to Burgundy and the Champagne. Excellent duck, game, freshwater fish. À la carte around 100–180F. Wines 50–300F.

Taverne Lyonnaise, rue Emile-Zola (25) 43.43.89: Lyonnaise cooking of Lyon dishes at very reasonable prices. Menu 40F; à la carte cheap. Shut Fri.; Aug.

Old town with many interests. Centre of hosiery trade for 470 years. Rich in works of art and buildings dating back to 12th century. After victory at Agincourt, Henry V of England married Catherine, daughter of King Charles VI of France in St Jean Church, Troyes, and became Regent of France. Troyes' magnificent cathedral was being built from 12th to 17th centuries and was still never finished.

St Laurent, rue Emile-Zola
(25) 43.14.89: 17th-century
hotel; comfortable old-style
décor; local dishes; Troyes
andouillette (chitterling
sausage), trout; reasonable
prices; menu 37–55F; rooms
50–145F.

St Vincent – railway station
buffet; always worth trying in
France. Menu 38–70F; cheap
carafe wine.

N77 St Florentin, D905 Tonnerre (76km)

St Florentin – L'Est, route de
Troyes (86) 35.10.35: good
local cooking; chicken in
Chablis; veal escalope in
cream sauce; snails; menu
45–100F; rooms 50–120F;
shut Dec.–March.

At Venizy, 4.5km from St
Florentin on D129 – Moulin
des Pommerats (86)
35.08.04: no hotel or
restaurant in all my books
has attracted such constant
enthusiasm from readers as
this pretty old watermill. Not
just the good food and wine
attracts them, nor the
riverside garden, but
ambience created by Paul
Reumaux d'Equainville. Paul
should understand the
eccentricities of the British.
He fought as an RAF officer
1940–45. Everything
splendid, from quail with
bilberries to terrines,
Burgundy snails, veal in
cream and trout from the
river. Good wine list. Lovely
Chaorce cheese (soft,
creamy, fruity); menu 75–
104F (also children's menu);

St Florentin is a small
industrial centre, but
interesting. At the meeting of
two rivers and a canal, it is
fishermen's country; church
with Renaissance stained
glass.

Route then follows Burgundy
canal to Tonnerre – an old
town which deals in wine
and is surrounded by
vineyards and meadows. A
spring (Fosse Dionne) of
blue-green water is
traditionally used by locals
for washing their clothes
'whiter than white'.

Tonnerre was the birthplace
of Chevalier d'Eon, diplomat
and spy, who appeared
publicly as both a man and a
woman, died in London in
1810 and was buried in St
Pancras.

East (8km by N65) is
Château Tanlay, started in
1547 by the Coligny brothers,
Protestant leaders in the
Religious Wars, finished 1648
by a tax collector who went
broke doing it; moated, very

St Florentin, Tonnerre *continued*

rooms 175–260F. Shut Sun. evening, Mon. out of season, but try telephoning. Member Châteaux Hôtels Indépendants.

Tonnerre – L'Abbaye St Michel (86) 55.05.99: historic Benedictine abbey; expensive, superb, beautiful; excellent traditional cooking. Menu 140F; rooms 300–400F. Shut Mon. off-season.

attractive, contains strange allegoric painting of Catholic and Protestant rivalry.

D905 Montbard (45km)

Hôtel l'Ecu, rue A. Carré (80) 92.11.66: comfortable, 17th century with Louis XVI dining room; wide range of menus; try coq au vieux Bourgogne; meurette de boeuf (in sauce of red wine, bacon, onions, carrots, mushrooms); chicken livers in raspberry vinegar; menu 55–140F; rooms 90–180F (all with bath or shower, wc); Logis de France.

Winding, pleasant route alongside Burgundy canal. This is Burgundy châteaux country. One castle not to miss is Ancy-le-Franc – a masterpiece of classical Renaissance and landmark in the history of architecture. Rooms are sumptuously decorated and the furniture, books, frescos and ancient tapestries are magnificent (18km from Tonnerre).

Côte d'Or, rue Carnot (80) 92.01.77: another Logis, known for its cooking; good grills; menu 39–95F; rooms 90–154F.

At Montbard, Comte de Buffon knocked down a castle on a hill, built a simple study in a park, and wrote his *Natural History* (first volume 1749). Several of his other buildings are still there. Nearby is the superb medieval abbey of Fontenay. A paper factory after the Revolution, it was completely restored after 1902.

D905 Dijon (81km)

Pré aux Clercs et Trois Faisans, pl Libération (80) 67.11.33: a famous French gourmet guide-writer has criticised Trois Faisans, especially for sauces. My family and my readers have had better luck. Still excellent value for one of the best in the region; typical simple but superb Burgundian cuisine; try braised ham with morilles (fungi) in cream; duck drumsticks (cuisse) stewed in Fleuri wine; duck pie. Menu 80–120F. Outstanding wine list. Shut Sun. evening. Also grill (over wood), called La Chasse Royale.

Hôtel du Nord, rue Liberté (80) 30.55.20: for four generations this hotel, rich in solid, polished wood, has kept its solid tradition of serving Burgundian dishes, traditionally cooked – tripes au rosé Marsannay, coq au vin, boeuf Bourguignon, rognons Dijonnaise, poire Dijonnaise – and served old Burgundy wines (currently from 1926 vintage onwards

Victor Hugo called Dijon 'delightful' and it still is. Outstanding for food even in this gastronomic area of France; so many interesting things to see that it deserves at least one overnight stay. The chiming clock of St Michel started in the 17th century with a blacksmith. Now he has a wife and two children. Among the many museums worth seeing, even if you are not a museum lover, is the Beaux Arts, in the palace of Charles de Valois: one of the most popular in France, with spectacular old carvings, and including royal tombs, as well as paintings. Among many fine old streets, rue des Forges is outstanding. Square Darcy, named after British engineer who gave Dijon clean water supply, is charming; the polar bear statue is by François Pompon, great animal artist. Superb Gastronomic Fair in November. You can buy Dijon mustard cheaply in

Dijon
continued

30–750F). Happy memories of dinner here during long-past Dijon Gastronomic Fair with great British gourmet Robin McDouall of the Travellers' Club. Menu 75–100F; rooms 75–195F. Shut early Jan.

plastic buckets. Dijon produces 85 per cent of France's cassis (blackcurrant liquor). Refreshing apéritif, Kir (cassis and white wine) was named after Canon Kir, mayor of Dijon and wartime Resistance leader. He served it at functions to promote sale of cassis for his town.

N74 Gevrey Chambertin (12km)

Rôtisserie du Chambertin (80) 34.33.20: Mme Céline Menneveau is generally rated best lady restaurateur in France. All is magnificent – food, service, décor, wine cellar (presided over by her husband, a brilliant buyer). Genius costs money – at least 150F, probably 250F for a meal. Then you have the problem of deciding which of her magnificent dishes to choose. Shut Sun. evening, Mon. Booking essential.

Aux Vendanges de Bourgogne, route Beaune (80) 34.30.24: modern; pleasant; excellent value; very good salmon, trout, coq au vin; well-chosen wine list; menu 44–79F; rooms 57–140F. Shut Mon.; Feb.

The great wine route starts. It would take a week to taste even a fraction of the good wines, but with a strong-willed or teetotal driver and a few diversions, you could stop at your favourite villages. Chambertin (Champ de Bertin) was Napoleon's favourite tipple, but the Corsican mixed it with water. ('St Peter', wrote Hilaire Belloc, 'I cannot remember the name of the village, the girl, or even what we ate for dinner. But, my God, the wine was Chambertin!') And many still call it 'King of Wines'. Do try Clos-de-Bèze if possible – the original wine produced by Bèze Abbey

Les Terroirs, route Dijon (80) 34.30.76: pleasant 3-star Logis; pretty interior; no restaurant but make and sell own wines; rooms 80–160F. Shut 23 Dec.–15 Jan.

Richebourg, rue Richebourg (80) 34.30.37: simple, rustic with good young chef trying to be creative (goat's milk cheese – chavignol – with fish). Good value; menu 50–80F. Shut Sun. evening, Mon.

monks. Bertin bought the field next door. Biggest production now is of Charmes Chambertin. Castle (10th century) worth visiting.

N74 Chambolle-Mussigny (5km on small road to right)

Passing Morey-St-Denis, whose wines we once knew as Gevrey and Chambolle. Best known is Clos de Tart, owned by Mommessin family since 1932 – pale, fruity wine drunk youngish. Try also Clos de la Roche and Clos de la Bussière. Chambolle-Mussigny, whose church has paintings of saints, produces wine almost in Chambertin class. Try Bonnes Mares; vineyard overlaps into Morey. Or, if in love, drink Les Amoureuses.

N74 Vougeot (3km)

Cistercian monks (Trappists) originally planted this vineyard at Vougeot and in the 14th century it was surrounded by a stone wall to protect it from raiders in the 100 Years' War. Now there are sixty-nine owners, making a choice of wines difficult, but all are very drinkable. The 16th-century château was bought in 1944 by the Confrérie des

Vougeot
continued

Chevaliers du Testevin, an organisation begun to publicise Burgundy wines; in scarlet and gold robes they hold banquets to enrol new members. At other times you can visit the château. It is spectacularly illuminated on weekends in July and August.

So highly regarded is Clos de Vougeot that the Revolutionary Colonel Bisson started a tradition by ordering his troops to 'present arms' as they passed the vineyard. Tasting at La Grande Cave on N74.

N74 Vosne-Romanée (6km)

From here come magnificent wines: deep, rich Romanée-Conti; Richbourg, so easy to drink that you tend to quaff it; les Grands Echézeaux, more delicate, for languid enjoyment. Romanée is called Queen of Wines – alas, a costly Queen.

N74 Nuits St Georges (3km)

Des Cultivateurs (80) 61.10.41: remarkable Relais Routiers, also 2-star hotel; comfortable bedrooms, pleasant dining room; charming terrace. Used by wine workers; fine wine list 25–150F; specialities: trout meunière, chicken chasseur, snails; couscous in winter. Menu 40–55F; rooms 65F to 4-person rooms at 164F. Sound-proofed. Shut Sun. after mid-day.

A little town almost as important as Beaune in the wine trade. Even has an hospice (founded 1692, caring for old folk) owning vineyards, given by the charitable or conscience-stricken and holding wine sales yearly. Until controls tightened, phoney 'Nuits' sold in Britain spoiled its repute. Prémaux wines are good, reliable, strong. Red wines need time to mature. White are scarcer but good. Some lesser wine made into sparkling red Burgundy – ugh! Street narrow and busy. Park and explore side streets.

N74 Aloxe Corton (18km – just off N74)

At Chorey-les-Beaune, just off N74 before reaching Beaune – Le Bareuzai (80) 22.02.90: dull modern building with handsome snug interior; large fireplace, wood-fire grill; restaurant run by wine producers and merchants, with big wine cave nearby in village and cellars still equipped with ancient wooden vats for production. Excellent restaurant with simple menu at 44F, excellent four-course at 83F, special menu with half bottle of '79 Beaune or white Burgundy for 130F and super 5-course feast for 160F. One chef expert on Burgundian cooking, the other on fish and modern dishes. Mouthwatering wine list. Shut first 5 weeks of year. No rooms but tied up with Host. de Bretonnière (see Beaune).

At foot of Montagne de Corton whose vineyards climb to a wooded hilltop. Wines were made at Aloxe for Charlemagne in 775 and it produces both red and white 'grand-cru' wines. Legend says that Charlemagne's wife nagged him because his favourite red wine stained his white beard, so he ordered part of the vineyard to be planted to produce white wine. The red (Aloxe Corton) is the best wine of Côte de Beaune, full blooded and fit for an emperor. Corton-Charlemagne ranks with Puligny-Montrachet as the finest white Burgundy. Voltaire lapped up the red – while serving his guests with Beaujolais! Le Corton red is outstanding, keeps up to 25 years. Top growth wines do not use word 'Aloxe'.

N74 Beaune (3km)

Central, rue Victor Millot (81) 24.77.24: after following this route, one of Britain's leading chefs told me that Robert Cuny offered some of the best *value* meals he had ever tasted. Very Burgundian – lots of cream and wine in sauces. Superb dishes on dearest menu like feuilletés (puff pastry cases) filled with salmon in tomato and cream sauce, sole in cress cream sauce, all covered in Aligote wine sauce. Excellent fish terrines; cheeses; pastries. Menu 70–120F; rooms 65–210F. Shut mid Nov.–31 March.

A lot to see in a smallish town, including the Hospice and Hôtel-Dieu (another hospital), both medieval, both with fine tapestries and other works of art and both kept in funds by the famous annual sale of wines from their vineyards ('biggest charity auction in the world'). Worth a walk round the old ramparts, a visit to the wine museum in the residence of the Dukes of Normandy, which includes a fine modern Arbusson tapestry by Jean Lurçat and some superb old glass, and, of course, a visit to a *cave* (list from tourist

Beaune
continued

Au Raisin de Bourgogne, route Dijon (80) 24.69.48: young Alain Billard offers an alternative to traditional Burgundian dishes. Some good ideas – try pot au feu de la mer – and outstanding sauces. But I confess, when in Beaune, I like to eat Burgundian! Wine list is local. Menu 80F (includes wine), 90F. Rooms 64–160F. Shut Weds. out of season; 15 Dec.–31 Jan.

Hostellerie de Bretonnière, faubourg Bretonnière (80) 22.15.77: comfortable bed and breakfast hotel tied to Le Bareuzai restaurant on N74 (see under Aloxe Corton earlier). Pleasant garden, private parking; bar. Rooms 74–148F.

office opposite Hôtel-Dieu). Excellent swimming pool in town, amid rose beds. Painting of *Last Judgement* by Van der Weyden in Hôtel-Dieu is magnificent. Forget those cheaper Beaunes bottled in Britain and try the real thing here. Beaune is the best wine for rich meals.

Pommard (6km S) is charming village with château which gives tastings. Wine should be deep rich red, fruity and soft.

D970 through Verdun-sur-le-Doubs (22km) on to Mervans, then D996 to Louhans (39km) (61km total)

Turn left off D970 at St Loup on to D183; just past Chaublanc – Moulin d'Hauterive (85) 91.55.56: (postal address 71350 St Gervais en Vallière): well worth 7km detour for hideaway with true *calme*. Pretty converted watermill; very comfortable; good cooking; a member of Relais du Silence – 'Calme, Tranquilité, Repos' (Quiet, Peace, Rest). Menu 70–140F; wines 53–300F; rooms 170F. Shut Sun. evening, Monday out of season; 15 Dec.–15 Jan.

A little-used route through river valleys. Verdun-sur-le-Doubs has a lovely tree-lined square facing two rivers. Louhans is a charming, photogenic little town at the meeting of two rivers; quiet except on market days when farmers bring in butter, eggs and poultry. Grand-Rue has fine arcaded houses of 17th and 18th centuries. The old hospital (Hôtel-Dieu) has a collection of glass (glasses, flagons, and Spanish and Moorish pottery). Just off Nouilly-Louhans road is the beautiful 17th-century Château of Pierre and park.

Louhans has a few reasonable restaurants and some cheap market eating places. Good value is:

Cheval Rouge, rue d'Alsace (85) 75.21.42: best restaurants in France get their chickens from this area, so try poulet à la crème; good salmon too; menu 36–73F; rooms 55–70F. Shut Sun. evening, Mon. out of season.

D996 Bourg en Bresse (56km)

An area producing splendid fresh dairy products and poultry, so mostly the cooking is simple, the result often delectable. Chicken is usually cooked in cream and white wine. Bleu de Bresse cheese is another local speciality.

Mail, ave du Mail (74) 21.00.26: though Auberge Bressane facing the church is more famous than Mail, it is dearer. Roger Charolles roasts chicken splendidly; his snails are good, his frogs' legs very good, his fish excellent; fish 'as it arrives fresh' – salmon, turbot, sea bass, sole, brill, red mullet. French experts say that cuisine here never falters. Wines from 40F, strong in Burgundy and Bordeaux. Menu 60–120F; pretty garden; pleasant bedrooms 65–130F. Shut part July, Jan.; Sun. evening; Mon.

Revermont, rue Ch. Robin (74) 22.66.53: nice simple corner restaurant with rooms; popular with locals

One can tire of looking at old churches in France, but the church at Brou, suburb of Bresse, is one of the prettiest – a meeting of Gothic, Flamboyant and Renaissance design, dainty rather than magnificent; the choir stalls, carved by the best local craftsmen, are remarkable. One shows a master enthusiastically beating the bare bottom of a pupil. The nearby tombs were carved by craftsmen brought from Flanders, Italy and Germany. Superb windows.

The story of the Brou Monastery is, alas, too long and complicated to tell here, but worth reading – a story of an orphan princess used for political power from babyhood, divorced, widowed but so intelligent that she became Regent of the Netherlands and Franche-Comté – wise, liberal, loved by the Comptois people: Marguerite of Austria, daughter of Emperor Maximilian.

| Bourg en Bresse *continued* | for good cooking of Bressane dishes; value; menu 30–87F; rooms 50–80F; shut Mon. | Bresse makes fine rustic furniture from cherry, pear and apple trees, and is the market for the great Bresse chickens and dairy produce. |

De France, pl Bernard (74) 23.30.24: real old 'Grand' hotel; restaurant popular locally; menu 55–78F; rooms 60–210F. Rest. shut Sun.

Savoie, rue Paul-Pioda (74) 23.29.24: good local cooking; choice of 5 menus 35–100F. Shut part August, Wed. evening, Thursday.

| N75 Pont d'Ain (19km) | Mas Pommier (2km N on N75) (74) 39.08.42: excellent value. Whole room devoted to 40 hors d'oeuvres dishes and choice of sausages hanging on wall. Try salmon; trout; quail with crayfish sauce or, of course, roast Bresse chicken. Menu 35, 42, 60, 83F. Rooms 35–70F. Shut Tues. evening, Weds. out of season. | From here you motor through the foothills of the Alps and some nice scenery. Lovely mountain scenery with a waterfall at Artemare (Cascade de Cerveyrieu). |

Alliés (34) 39.00.09: more good local cooking, plus good wines 28–180F. Menu 60–120F. Rooms 80–150F. Shut Friday evening, Thur. out of season; also Nov.

| N75 Ambérieu en Bugey (12km) N504 to Rossillon (37km) and then turn left on D904 to Artemare (50km) | Savoie (74) 38.06.90: recommended locally; menu 40–100F; cold buffet in evening; rooms 150–165F. |

At Lutheziev (from Artemare, 8km by D31 and D8) – Vieux Tilleul (79) 87.64.51: good traditional cooking of the region; weekday 38F menu is good value; other menus up to 170F. Fair range of wines. Shut Jan.

D904 to Culoz (15km) Ruffieux (4km) then D991 to Aix les Bains (20km)

Ruffieux – Château de Collanges, (79) 63.27.38: turreted manor, most attractive, beautifully furnished. A Châteaux de Tradition hotel (one of three Châteaux chains); silent, restful, nice garden, excellent service; Bourget lake nearby; try salmon trout; perch; all freshwater fish, especially crayfish. Menu 90–130F; rooms 180–275F (all with bath, wc). Shut 1 Nov.–15 March.

At Aix – Hôtel Dauphinois et Nivolet, ave Tresserve (79) 61.22.56: attractive old hotel with pleasant terrace for dinner on warmer nights; nice garden, reliable cooking; confit of hare, beef en brioche, good freshwater fish. Menu 60–125F; rooms 100–185F; one of twelve Logis de France in Aix. Shut 30 Nov.–1 March.

Lakeside roads with lovely views of distant mountains and Dent du Chat across the water of Lake Bourget, largest lake in France. Aix is still one of the most fashionable spas in France. It even has a bust of Queen Victoria, who spent the spring of 1885 here. Two sulphur springs are for treating rheumatism, two others less sulphuric for mineral waters. There are two casinos, lovely gardens, good sailing, lake trips and the Fauré Museum with fine modern paintings – Cézanne, Degas, Pissarro, Corot, Rodin (watercolours). To the French, Aix remains the scene of the great love affair between the poet Lamartine and Elvire, the girl from French Caribbean married to an old man and in Aix to cure TB. She died in Paris

Aix les Bains
continued

Hostellerie le Manoir, rue George I (79) 61.44.00: attractive, restful; like country house in pleasant grounds; charming bedrooms of varying sizes. Try lavaret (Savoy lake fish like salmon) or real salmon; good straightforward cooking of good fresh ingredients; menu 75–110F; rooms 100–200F. Shut Xmas–1 Feb.

International Hôtel Rivollier, ave Ch. de Gaulle (79) 35.21.00: a period piece, very pre-war, run with old-fashioned courtesy by same family for 75 years; old-style touches such as silver platters; huge dining room; classic dishes; menu 65–130F; nice bedrooms 60–200F.

Auberge du Monument, square A. Boucher (79) 35.07.38: in market place, simple restaurant, good value; copious portions; quick service; menu 34–67F; simple rooms 45–55F. Shut 20 Dec.–1 March.

La Mère Michaud, rue de Genève (79) 35.06.03: super little typical bistro-hotel; quiet shady garden at back; thermal baths available; good family cooking; menu 48–80F; wines from 16F; rooms 80–100F (half (20) with bath, wc).

the next year (1817) and he wrote a passionate poem 'Lac' when she did not rejoin him at Aix.

Boats take you to Abbaye de Hautecombe; catch the 8.30am boat in summer to join abbey's Gregorian chant. Otherwise drive to hear chant at other services.

**D991
Chambéry
(16km)**

Roubatcheff, rue Théâtre
(79) 33.24.91: small, friendly
restaurant run by father and
son; Michelin star; not
surprisingly, Caucasian
dishes like chachlick and
borsch (the family is of
Russian descent). Do try the
gâteau of fresh salmon and
crayfish; superb desserts
with huge choice; fine wine
cellar. Very pricey. 'Little'
menu 90F; others to 240F.

La Chaumière, rue Denfort
(79) 33.16.26: nearer to my
price and good value. Patron-
chef Alain Boisson cooks
traditionally and very well.
Good lamb; duck liver; menu
50–95F; shut Wed. evening;
Sun.; 8 Aug.–1 Sept.

Savoyard, pl. Monge (79)
33.36.55: mountain-chalet
style, terrace; local Savoyard
dishes – fondue, raclette,
potée Savoyard (soup thick
with meat and veg); diots
(pork and veg sausage
cooked in wine). Good value;
menu 38–85F; house-wine
19F; rooms 52–58F. Shut
Sun.

Le Tonneau, rue St Antoine
(79) 33.78.26: had a facelift;
funny wall drawings;
splendid mountain meals of
Savoyard dishes; several
menus: 30, 38F (weekdays),
45, 65, 85F; all good value;
lavaret from the lake; diots;
genuine gratin dauphinois
(potato slices baked in
cream); big choice of
cheeses including Beaufort,

Once capital of the Duchy of
Savoy, then an independent
state. It did not join France
until 1860. Chambéry is
dominated by the castle of
the Dukes of Savoy, rebuilt in
the 15th century and restored
later after fires. You can visit
it in summer. Magnificent
views up here from outside
or inside. It is an attractive
old town, with narrow
arcaded streets surrounded
by wide boulevards. It is on
the banks of the river Leysse,
and is the main centre for
Savoy mountain excursions.

Along N542, 2km, is Les
Charmettes, a truly charming
country house where
Rousseau lived for two years
with Mme de Warens; he
grew flowers, she kept bees.

Chambéry
continued

tomme, goat and superb
reblochon local creamy
cheese; house-wine 16F.
Shut Monday; part Aug.

**N6 St Jean de
Maurienne
(71km)**

The route to Modane is up
and down but broad and
easy with fine scenery. The
old town St Jean de
Maurienne has yet another
cathedral (11th to 13th
centuries).

**N6 Modane
(31km)**

Perce-Neige, cours J. Jaurès
(79) 05.00.50: good value;
menu 44 (weekdays), 58F;
rooms 108–155F. Shut early
May; 1–15 Oct.

Voyageurs, facing station (79)
05.01.39: menu 44–90F; shut
Sun.

Fréjus road tunnel after
Modane (toll: cars 36–76F)
into Italy; road at Italian end
still needs some attention
(autumn 1982).

Good-weather alternative is
to drive 23km to
Llanslebourg for the Mont
Cenis pass to Susa (easy
widish road but surfaces a bit
dodgy in places). Lovely
route.

Route 4
Calais to Geneva

Traditional French cooking to many Britons means the cuisine of Ile de France near Paris, Provence, and perhaps Burgundy. Route 4 increases our knowledge of provincial French cooking. The Pas de Calais is influenced by the cream, cider and fresh fish of Normandy. Inland Picardy has a Flemish flavour, with duck, freshwater fish (especially trout and eels), creamy leek tart (flamiche), multitudes of sausages and cooking in beer and Geneva gin – solid food rather than subtle.

Champagne cooking is underestimated and is none the worse for Ile de France and Burgundy influences. Lamb, pork (excellent charcuterie and even breaded baked pig's trotters). Crayfish and chicken are cooked in still champagne (a nice apéritif) and some fine dishes in red Bouzy wine. When you get home, do not attempt those dishes in *fizzy* champagne – a costly error. Pike soufflé (pain à la rein) with crayfish sauce is surprisingly tasty. Brie came originally from here; chaource is a superb creamy cheese.

In Burgundy they have turned local dishes into gourmet feasts. The Dijon area is known for magnificent beef, game, freshwater fish (try pochouse – mixed fish stewed in wine), coq au Chambertin (a snob coq au vin), snails, gingerbread (pain d'épice) and spicy wine mustard used variously in sauces (usually with cream and called 'à la Dijonnaise'). Meurettes is a spicy red wine sauce with shallots.

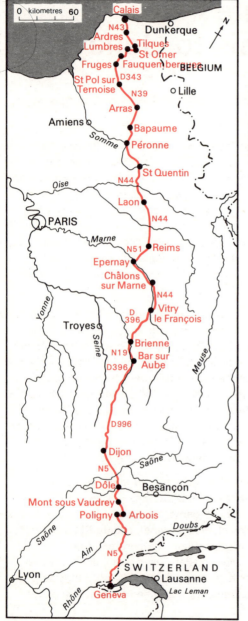

Calais
N43
Ardres
Lumbres   Tilques
              St Omer
Fruges   Fauquembergues
St Pol sur   D343
Ternoise   N39
    Arras
        Bapaume
        Péronne
            St Quentin
    N44
        Laon
            N44
        N51 Reims
    Epernay
    Châlons
    sur Marne
            N44
        D   Vitry
        396 le François
    Brienne
N19   Bar sur
D396   Aube

    D996

    Dijon
N5   Saône
    Dôle
Mont sous Vaudrey
Poligny   Arbois

    N5
        SWITZERLAND
            Lausanne
    Geneva   Lac Leman

Calais
0 kilometres 60

Dunkerque
BELGIUM
Lille
Amiens
Somme
Oise
PARIS
Marne
Yonne
Troyes
Seine
Meuse
Besançon
Saône
Ain
Doubs
Lyon
Rhône

Calais
PARIS
Geneva

The blackcurrant apéritif Crème de Cassis can be served with white wine (Kir) or dry white vermouth.

I once attended Dijon's annual Gastronomic Festival and came home heavier and happier. I found myself breakfasting with a girl I did not know but seemed to know, on the wall of a fountain which was spouting red wine, eating splendid sausage from a stall in the square!

The route north of Paris is surprisingly direct yet misses most industrial areas and heavier traffic roads. It is planned to pass through lesser-known, attractive areas, like the hill country south of St Omer, the lovely countryside of Aisne with its beautiful old hilltop city of Laon, the Champagne and its vineyards, and the delightful and almost unknown country around the Aube valley. You can join it from Boulogne at St Omer; from Dieppe or Le Havre at Arras, Bapaume or St Quentin.

Try to leave time for a visit to a champagne house in Dijon or Epernay. You could return along the Burgundy wine road to Dijon, stopping perhaps at Chambertin.

A suggested return route nearer to Paris: Chaumont, Troyes, Crépy-en-Valois, Senlis, Chantilly, Beauvais.

Route 4
Calais to Geneva

Calais

La Feuillandine, place d'Armes (21) 97.32.57: when the famous Hamiot family sold their brasserie in Boulogne, Dad joined Grandad at the gastronomic Atlantic in Wimereux; Grandson Eric started this simple, attractive little restaurant in Calais; already making an impact with menu 'marché' – fresh ingredients bought daily, short menu of dishes to fit. Mother Jacqueline shares cooking. Menu 51F; carte reasonable; shut Sunday.

Moulin à Poivre, rue Neuve (21) 96.22.32: Gerard Carette's restaurant started six years ago as answer to Calais' prayer. Now a little variable – one meal excellent, next indifferent. Simple menu at 40F good value; otherwise à la carte. Shut Sunday; Mon. lunchtime.

Le Channel, boulevard Résistance (21) 34.42.30: another 6-year-old; I ate there in its first week; now very popular with British tourists; service efficient,

Signposts from the ferry encourage you to hurry round the town but there are genuine local grocers, greengrocers and wine shops; many are around place d'Armes, a medieval square until destroyed in the last war; rebuilt in utility style. Good cheese shop across square offering 200 cheeses. Locals shop in streets higher up, beyond the railway station. Outside the Flemish town hall is Rodin's statue to the burghers who defied the English under Edward III; on the islet in the harbour the Green Jackets (Rifle Brigade) stood against the Nazis in 1940. War museum in German naval HQ bunker include British wartime newspapers.

Hypermarket at Marck sells *almost* everything. You can wheel your trolley into the café and have crêpes or coffee and brandy, which we cannot yet do in our local Tescos. Large beach used by locals, not many Britons.

food reliable; good fish; menu 33, 52, 110F; shut Sun. evening; Tues. off season. 15 Dec.–15 Jan.

Coq d'Or, pl. d'Armes (21) 34.79.05: back in favour locally; new owners settled down; several menus 45–100F; 77F good value; shut Weds.

Sole Meunière, boulevard Résistance (21) 34.43.01: once one of the best fish restaurants in N. France; now smaller, cheaper, but still fairly good for fish; menu 39–100F; shut Mon.; Sun. evening out of season; 20 Dec.–26 Jan.

At Blériot Plage, 2km on D940 – Des Dunes (21) 34.54.30: little old inn has sprouted large modern dining-room; excellent cooking; try salmon rillettes; sole in champagne; sea food; menu 38–140F; rooms (being renovated) 78–105F; shut Mon.; early Oct.; Feb.

From Blériot Plage, 2km on D940, Blériot took off from the beach on first channel flight in 1909. A memorial also to Lambert, who ditched in the Channel earlier and was picked up nonchalantly smoking a cigarette.

**N43 Ardres
(17km)**

**RELAIS DU
SILENCE**

Grand Hôtel Clément, pl. Mar. Leclerc (21) 35.40.66: like many British and French of my generation, I have watched it grow from pretty Logis to gastronomic Relais de Silence; cooking better than ever but prices getting ahead of me. I realise that Paul Coolen would never lower standards even during recession but my bank manager doesn't! Flower-decked building; attractive garden for apéritifs and coffee; cosy, chintzy bedrooms; menu 100–220F; rooms 115–180F. Shut Mon. low season, 15 Jan.–15 Feb.

La Chaumière (21) 35.41.24: pleasant bed and breakfast hotel; 75–145F.

At Brêmes, 1km on D231 – La Bonne Auberge (21) 35.41.09: country inn run by nice people; I have had good meals; most readers very happy; three were not. Good trout; ficelle Picarde (pancake

N43 is still a dull, crowded road. But off it, Ardres is a quiet village; network of waterways around it. Alternative route, but narrower, bumpier, on D127 to Guines (historic little town – English frontline HQ when we owned Calais; Ardres was French HQ), on to D231 through Brêmes to Ardres. This passes the Field of Cloth of Gold, where Henry VIII met Francis I of France in an ostentatious display of wealth and pomp, to discuss an alliance. Like most summit conferences, it got nowhere.

From Ardres, to avoid the N43, I often take D224 and wander on 'white' roads through Tourneheim Forest to St Omer (see Michelin map 51). Complicated, narrow roads, takes time, but rewarding.

stuffed with cream, ham,
cheese); tarte tatin (upside
down apple pie); menu
42.50–100F; rooms 62–100F
(good value). Shut Mon.,
Sun. evening in winter.

At Guines – Lion d'Or in
main square is old, simple
restaurant which looks left
over from 1914–18 war;
menu 39–65F.

**N43 Tilques
(18km)**

Vert Mesnil (21) 98.28.99:
whole image of this former
priest's seminary has
changed rapidly from a quiet
country hideaway run by a
young chef to an hotel with
small conference centre and
large dining room in former
barn. Dining room has
excellent service, very good
meals. Menu 60–130F; wines
30–100F; rooms all have bath
190–320F. Nice lawns, lake,
tennis court.

**N43 St Omer
(5km)**

Comte du Luxembourg, rue
C. de Luxembourg (21)
38.10.09: I have not tried it,
but was recommended
locally for value; new patron-
chef; traditional cooking;
menu 35–75F; rooms 60–
120F; shut Sun.; Mon. lunch
in winter.

Le Cygne, rue Caventon (21)
98.20.52: fine old building,
elegant dining room; known
for freshwater fish, duck,
fresh vegetables; menu 60F
(4-courses); shut Tues.
evening, Sat. lunch.

Centre of an area of
waterways and gardens
which lures painters, it has
some fine merchants' houses
of the 16th and 17th
centuries. Rue de l'Escugarie
holds Notre-Dame, a former
cathedral of the 13th century
with same period statue of
Christ and tomb of St Omer.
Good fine arts museum with
works by Flemish, Dutch and
French masters, lovely
tapestries, ceramics, mosaics,
ivories; pleasant boat trips
(½-hour) from near station
along garden-lined canals

St Omer
continued

and forest of Clairmarais, with reserve for migrating herons. The park has a good swimming pool and open-air theatre (summer). For bizarre nostalgia, one of the first German rocket bases for attacking Britain (at Wizernes, 4km on N28).

D208 to Wisques, D212, N42 Lumbres (13km)

Wisques – La Sapinière (21) 38.14.59: in a neat old white house, the Mesmacie family offer simple bedrooms and good traditional French cooking; good value; try lamb, salmon, quail, and nice fish quiche; menu 45F; carte reasonable; wines from good Côte de Blaye for only 28F to '59 St Emilion 125F; some criticism of table service; rooms 55–115F; shut Sun. evenings, Mon.

Benedictine abbey at Wisques in a château and a hilltop building: ancient (15th century) and modern (1953) architecture; Gregorian chant at 9.45am mass. Lovely hill country.

Lumbres – Moulin de Mombreux (21) 39.62.44: very difficult to find, but too many do, so book! Lovely watermill in unlikely spot near factory chimneys (unseen once in mill grounds). We found it 16 years ago when Jean Marc Gaudry slipped in quietly from l'Oasis at Napoules (3-star Michelin) and offered true gastronomic cooking in remote Pas de Calais village. It remains a revelation. Magnificent rich, thick, 'alcoholic' French sauces; everything beautiful, especially vegetables. Little choice; menu 100, 160F; rooms vary in size and price: 55–100F; shut Sun. evening, Mon.

Trou Normand on N42 (21) 39.63.65: village inn; wood and checked tablecloths; country dishes – trout, guinea fowl, rabbit, local chickens; menu 50–75F; simple rooms from 45F; shut Sun. evening, Mon.

Lumbres, on river l'Aa; old squares, narrow streets; trout fishing but also paper mills, cement works.

D193, D225, D195 Fauquembergues (14km)

Off D225 at Clété – Truite d'Or: nice auberge with 40F menu; good choice includes steak.

At Merck-St Lieven on D225, at trout farm with 40 ponds; see them thrash about when fed. Fauquembergues, typical little old market town with fine 13th-century church, is now missed by N42.

D928 Fruges
(10km)

Take D928 on to Ruisseauville (4km) and lane signposted to Azincourt – Agincourt – where in 1415 Henry V's small army beat a French army three times its size. Poignantly and simply marked by a cross; an Englishman should count himself accursed for not seeing it.

D928, D343
St Pol sur
Ternoise
(25km)

Catherinette, in suburb of St Michel (21) 03.12.42: lunch only – now a disco at night! Excellent value for families; lawns, children's playground; menu 30–40F (except Sun.); 75F (excellent value); wines 25–250F. Shut Feb.

N39 Arras
(34km)

This is Flanders, and that means Flemish cooking, often in beer or Geneva gin; with sausages, hotpots, delightful flans, and big portions.

Chanzy, rue Chanzy (21) 21.02.02: many readers delighted with this bustling, famous restaurant where you need a big appetite; the de Troy family are the real experts at Flemish cooking; local sausages flambés in Geneva gin; chicken in beer; wild rabbit casseroled in leeks; potée flamande (bacon, ham, sausage, potatoes); hochepot (beef, mutton, pork and veg); lovely Flemish leek flan; big choice of charcuterie; huge wine cellar cut out of rock with

Deceptive appearance, for Arras is interesting. Almost destroyed in the 1914–18 war, much of it was rebuilt as before, such as the 15th-century town hall which has a bust of a well known local lad, Robespierre, the French Revolutionary leader; rooms are furnished in 16th-century style. La Grande Place and place des Héros have old-style arcaded buildings, and Grande Place buildings have coats of arms of craftsmen and merchants. Good market.

At the Citadel is a moving memorial to 200 French Resistance fighters shot by Nazis, and alongside the graves of 35,000 British killed in World War I. Vimy ridge,

100,000 bottles; wines dating from 1868; won Lauréat Mondial for world's best wine card in '79. Wines 20–2000F; menu 53, 110F (gastronomic); rooms 70–175F.

Ambassadeur (21) 23.29.80: only station buffet with a Michelin star! Delightful décor; superb cooking; reasonable prices. Try herrings à la Flamande, ham with leeks; duck; pannequet (pancakes); turbotin (small turbot). Menu 65 (weekdays); 100F; shut Sun. evenings.

Inter Hôtel Moderne, by station (21) 23.39.57: very comfortable bed and breakfast hotel, with brasserie beneath; all rooms with bath, wc; rooms 140–200F.

where 75,000 Canadians died fighting in 1917, is 8km along N25. A huge, impressive memorial, it is sombre and frightening when you consider the confusion and life-wastage of the campaign of that year.

N17 D944, N29 through Bapaume, Péronne, to St Quentin (70km)

At Péronne – Hostellerie des Remparts, rue Beaubois (22) 84.01.22: delightfully attractive with flowers, coloured blinds outside; solid comfort within; meals for most purses; terrace for good weather eating; nice cosy inn. Menu 45, 48, 60, 90, 100F; rooms 80–150F. Shut early August.

At Neuville St Amand, 3km SE St Quentin on D12 – Château de Neuville (23) 68.41.82: another delightful restaurant, deserving its Michelin star for classic French cooking, and wine list from France; towered château not exactly pretty

How to restore your spirits is a fine park called Champs-Élysées built on devastated battlefields; also a lagoon beside the Somme for boating and with a beach. How sensibly the French make beaches beside rivers and lakes.

**Péronne,
St Quentin**
continued

but pleasant grounds for
summer eating and inside,
restaurant divided cleverly
for intimate dining and views
over garden. Known for
excellent service. Menu 90F
(weekdays); 120F (Sundays).
Shut Sun. and Wed.
evenings; all Monday;
August.

**N44 Laon
(46km)**

Bannière de France, rue F.
Roosevelt (23) 23.21.44:
friendly old inn with lots of
polished wood and cosy
rooms; meals excellent
value; try terrine of fish and
crab (tourteaux); scallop
soup; kidneys in Bouzy wine;
good honest boeuf
Bourguignon; I love this inn
and so do many readers.
Charming atmosphere. Menu
50 (includes wine), 85, 130F.
Well-chosen wines. Rooms
61–210F. Shut 20 Dec.–10
Jan.

Angleterre, blvd Lyon (in
lower town) (23) 23.04.62:
modern hotel, much nicer
inside; comfort, most
pleasant décor; reliable
cooking at sensible prices;
menu 45, 75, 130F; rooms
65–190F.

La Petite Auberge, boulevard
Brossolette (lower town) (23)
23.51.79: bargain rotisserie,
using wood-fire cooking;
good steaks, ham steaks,
veal cutlets; menu 37, 51,
79F. Shut Sat.

A delightful old city, once
capital of France (4th to 9th
centuries) set high on a steep
hill, with magnificent views,
especially from medieval
ramparts; worth an overnight
stop to explore and enjoy its
old buildings, streets, and
rampart walks; Cathedral of
Notre-Dame (12th century) is
one of the oldest Gothic
cathedrals in France. From
outside it is beautiful, inside
it is magnificent. There are
so many historic church
buildings in France that they
can set me yawning, but this
one is not to be missed.

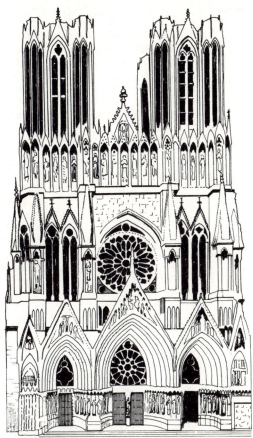

N44 Reims (47km)

Good restaurants mostly very dear (Boyer, ave d'Epernay, around 350F for a meal); too many tourist restaurants charging too much for mediocre cooking.

Restaurant Le Drouet, at Hôtel la Paix, rue Buirette (26) 40.04.08: 'Grand Hôtel' restaurant giving very good value, good service; menu 60–95F. Shut Sunday.

The kings of France used to be crowned here and I don't blame them. The cathedral can *really* be called a masterpiece; it was begun in 1211, damaged in world War I, restored in 1938, and it is beautiful. Let's face it, most of us don't go to Reims for church architecture; we go to visit the champagne cellars. You might decide to put off this pleasure until you reach Epernay; I don't; I visit one cellar in each town. For some

Reims
continued

Le Forum, pl. Forum (26) 47.56.87: cheap, good value; menu changes daily; specialises in grills. Choices in every course. All menus 4 course (cheese plus dessert); menu 38, 58, 63F (Sunday).

Climat de France, la Neuvillette (26) 09.62.73: quiet, in pretty setting; menu 41–64F; rooms 130–169F.

visits you need letters of introduction. Without introduction you can see these in Reims: Mumm – 34 rue du Champ de Mars; 45–minute tour. Veuve-Clicquot-Ponsardin – pl. des Droits de l'Homme: nice historic story of the Widow.

For Heidsieck Monopole – 83 rue Coquebert – you need letter from London agents Bouchard Ainé (13 Eccleston Street, London SW1): 8 million bottles maturing in 8 miles of caves! Don't worry, the tour is only round a section (45 mins). All offer tastings; hours vary but mostly 09.00–11.00, 14.00–16.30 weekdays. Clicquot opens Saturdays, Sundays except winter.

N31 west to Thillois, D26 to Gueux, Pargny, then local road to right to St–Lié and Villedommange; on to D26 to Sacy, Ecueil to Montchenot on N51 (27km)

A lovely run past motor racing circuit, winding through the Reims mountains and vineyards; magnificent views at St-Lié; from Sacy. The Black Pinot grapes are mostly grown here and in Marne Valley, the White Chardonnay mostly south of Epernay. Juice from both goes into the best champagne; it stays white because the juice of Pinot Noir is separated from skins before they impart their red colour; a little 'pink' champagne is made, and quite a lot of Blanc de Blancs from white grapes only. But as a member of the Mercier family said to me, 'Let us not talk about champagne – let us drink it.'

N51 Epernay (15km)

Chapon Fin, pl. Thiers (26) 51.40.03: good value; traditional regional cooking; known for coq au vin; in solid surroundings of old oak and old furniture; menu 40, 80F. Shut Sat.

Calmer than Reims; interesting wine history in Museum of Champagne. Visits to caves without introduction include: Moet et Chandon, ave de Champagne: founded 1743; largest cellars in the world (17½ miles of maturing bottles); museum has Napoleon's hat; he is on the important visitors' board – so are the Duke of Wellington, Blücher, the Duke of Hamilton (not Emma) and Khruschev.

Statue of Dom Pérignon (1638–1715) who perfected champagne making, and superb gardens; 4km north on N386 at Hautvilliers is a

Epernay
continued

Benedictine abbey, vineyards where Pérignon performed his miracle; owned since the Revolution by Moet.

Mercier, ave de Champagne: a mere 11 miles of galleries and an electric train to take you round; interesting chalk carvings, museum of wine presses and the largest wine cask in the world, made in 1889, and holding enough wine for 200,000 bottles, every party hostess should have one. There are millions of bottles maturing in these cellars. (Caves shut to public in winter.)

RD3 Chalons sur Marne (32km)

Aux Armes de Champagne, L'Epine, (8km on N3) (26) 68.10.43: 'cooking takes time', says the *carte*, 'quality of a dish and speed do not always go together'. How very true. And the food here is worth waiting for. Hugues Hoverd, the chef, came from La Mère Poulard at Mont-Saint-Michel. He tends towards Nouvelle Cuisine with simpler, lighter sauces most carefully cooked; menu 53, 96, 140F; formidable wine list with vintage champagnes; rooms 105–220F; shut 10 Jan.–15 Feb.

Angleterre, pl. Mon. Tissier (26) 68.21.51: same owners as Armes de Champagne; different chef and menu; even lighter 'nouvelle'. I like filet de boeuf au ratafia (unfermented grape juice and brandy). Attractive flowery terrace; menu 50, 92, 132F;

Here in 451 AD, in a bloody battle in which 200,000 were killed, Attila the Hun, 'scourge of God', was beaten by Romans, Visigoths and Franks; he fled to Hungary and turned his hordes onto Italy.

rooms 98–192F. Shut Sun.,
Mon. evenings; 15 Feb.–15
March.

N44 Vitry le François (32km)

Bon Séjour, fbg Léon
Bourgeois (26) 74.02.36:
good home cooking; Relais
Routiers weekday meal 28F
(excellent value), main menu
48F; rooms 55–80F; shut Sat.

D396 to Rosnay, Brienne-le-Château, at Maison Neuve take N19 to Bar-sur-Aube (66km)

Bar-sur-Aube – Commerce,
rue Nationale (25) 27.08.76:
Claude Paris has taken his
Logis to 1–star Michelin by
careful cooking of regional
dishes using top-quality
ingredients. Mostly grills and
roasts with light sauces, but
some diversions – brochette
of capon with nice curry
sauce and rice, fresh salmon
in red wine and green
peppers. Menu 80–105F;
rooms 75–180F. Shut Sun.
evenings, Mon. in winter,
early Jan.

Napoleon went to military
school in Brienne, when aged
9. He could still only speak
French in an Italian-Corsican
patois, but came top in
mathematics and military
exercises. Later he called the
region 'Ma Patrie'. In 1814 he
attacked a Prussian and
Russian army here. The
formidable château on the
hill is a hospital for
psychotherapy, and rather
naturally cannot be visited.
Bar is a charming little
market town beside a pretty
stretch of river, under
wooded and vine-covered
slopes. The route misses the
main traffic.

D396/D996 Dijon (114km)

See **Route 3**.

N5 Dôle (48km)

La Chaumière, ave de
Genève, D405 (84) 79.03.45:
most ambitious of Dôle's
four Logis de France: like a
big modern bungalow, local
reputation for good food;
good freshwater fish – try
pike soufflé; sandre (river
fish); local raw ham; good
cheeses. Menu 45–67F;

Louis Pasteur was born here,
son of a tanner, in a street
now named after him; there
is a small museum. Now an
industrial town, it is prettily
placed above river Doubs. A
long history of fighting for
independence against the
French kings; it was the first
town to be bombarded with

Dôle
continued

rooms good but pricey: 127–250F. Shut Sun. evening; Fri. eve., Sat. lunch out of season; 1 week June; 15 Dec.–15 Jan.

Buffet Gare (84) 82.00.48: one of those French station buffets with very good value meals. Menu 39–80F. Shut Thurs. evening.

howitzer shells – by Prince of Condé in 1636; but Dôle won, and the Archbishop, aged 80, watched the French retreat from the roof of the cathedral, thanked God, and dropped dead.

N5 to Mont sous Vaudrey D469 Arbois (37km)

De Paris, rue Hôtel de Ville (84) 66.05.67: André Jeunet looks exactly what a happy, plump French chef should be – and he is! He cooks truly gastronomic meals in rustic surroundings of former Carmelite monastery. Now his son Jean-Paul has joined him in the kitchen, so to André's famous fat hen in Arbois 'yellow' wine with morilles, his pike soufflé in thick crayfish sauce and his other classic sauces are added Jean-Paul's mousseline of green vegetables, mousse of broccoli and terrine of lamb with basil. Splendid local trout and salmon. Two readers actually *disappointed* with their meals – but outnumbered hundreds to two. Refreshing Jura wines. Menu 65, 120, 160F; rooms 68–170F. Shut Tues. out of season, 15 Nov.–15 March.

Hôtel des Messageries, rue Courcelles (N83) (84) 66.15.45: old, modernised comfortable bed and breakfast hotel, useful on way to or from Switzerland. Rooms 45–150F.

Arbois – centre of Jura wines; wine growers famous through centuries for independence and hot-headed actions; resenting the importance of Lyon, they declared their little city a republic in 1834. When the police demanded the revolt leaders, they said: 'We are *all* leaders.' Pasteur lived here, went to local primary school and college. His family home can be visited 15 April–30 Sept. His vineyard (2km on N83 towards Besançon), bought in 1874 and used for his experiments on fermentation, still produces good wine, drunk on special occasions.

La Finette, ave Pasteur (84)
66.06.78: old-style tavern run
that way. Three local dishes
only. Choice of starters;
menu 42–81F. Most local
wines, plus two Californian.

**N83 Poligny
(10km)**

De Paris, rue Travot (84)
37.13.87: attractively solid,
with flowered terrace; good
choice of menus 50–110F;
rooms 60–150F; shut Mon.
evenings, Tues. lunch, out of
season, 5 Nov.–5 Feb.

Fine views on this road of
the Jura plateau. Just past
Poligny, N5 passes La Culée
de Vaux – one of the valleys
used by the Romans as a
trading route. Lovely views
from Monts-de-Vaux.

**N5 Geneva
(98km)**

Route 5
Calais to Strasbourg
(for Germany and Austria)

Much of the route is in Alsace and Lorraine where food is good and solid rather than for gourmets – except that the pâté de foie gras of Strasbourg, which is superb to taste but sticks in many British gullets because the geese have been force fed.

Dairy products are used more lavishly in Lorraine. You will be surprised to find that the *local* quiche Lorraine contains no cheese. A delicious alternative is called quiche (or gâteau) au fromage blanc (cream cheese and bacon flan). Sauerkraut (choucroute) appears in many winter dishes in both areas (such as jambon à l'Alsacienne – ham with sauerkraut, Strasbourg sausage and potatoes).

Both provinces have a love of tarts, flans and pastry coverings. Even the delicate freshwater crayfish are often encased in pastry, though they are used in dozens of ways, including as a smooth pink sauce for covering other fish or chicken.

Alsace is a pork country, with plenty of good charcuterie, and goose country, with goose fat used for cooking. The German influence has made dumplings popular. Chickens are almost of the Bresse standard. Lorraine's German-inspired derentifleisch (smoked rib of beef) is very tasty.

Alsace wines come mostly from the French bank of the Rhine. They are made with similar grapes to the German wines (Riesling, Traminer and Sylvaner) but are dry for French palates, not sugared a little to suit Germans. They are strong. Even Muscat grapes are used to make dry white wines, not dessert wines. Moselle wines (quite different from German Mosel) are best when young. Lorraine's rosé wines are often called Vin Gris and are almost red! On labels, Zwicker means wines made with common grapes, Edelzwicker with nobler grapes.

Brandies are made from strawberries (fraise), raspberries (framboise), cherries (kirschwasser), pears (Poire William), plums (Quetsch) and greengages (Reine Claude).

An almost direct route from Calais or Boulogne. It avoids most of the northern industrial cities and takes you to some most attractive scenery, little known to the French themselves: the beautiful Meuse valley, with small roads running past rocks, ravines and hills, north of Hirson and Charleville to the Belgian border; the pleasant countryside of wooded hills and rivers between Longuyon and Metz; the hillocky road from St Avold to Saverne beneath the Vosges mountains. The industrial towns which you do meet, such as Arras and Metz, have special attractions and interests.

You could return on the more southerly route, back from Metz through Verdun, Reims in the Champagne and either through Compiègne (Route 3) or Laon (Route 4).

By crossing the Rhine into Germany at Strasbourg instead of going through Belgium and crossing into Germany at Aachen, you miss the industrial Ruhr and have a pleasant road to Stuttgart to join the motorway through to Frankfurt and Munich and into Austria.

Not many years ago you could find many British tourists in the northern towns through which this route passes – in Arras, Cambrai, Sedan, Metz. They were old soldiers of the 1914–18 war, returning to the battlefields where they had fought and their friends had died. Now most of them have joined their friends, and their sons make pilgrimages to Arnhem and the Normandy beaches. But to anyone with a sense of history these northern battlefields of France are still sadly dramatic and local museums deeply interesting. Read the histories of the towns and villages and you begin to understand the French better.

This route is 634km (393 miles). The RAC-suggested route is 601km (379 miles).

Route 5
Calais to Strasbourg

(for Germany and Austria)

Calais to St Omer See **Route 4.**

From St Omer N43 Aire-sur-la-Lys (18km)

Aire – Hostellerie des Trois Mousquetaires at Château de la Redoute (21) 39.01.11: my favourite grill in Europe; deservedly famous now, so book. Also pleasant bedrooms in gabled 19th-century mock château; pleasant grounds with lawns to river Lys and lake with swans and ducks. Open kitchen and wood-fired grill, so you can see Marcel Venet and son Philipe cooking your splendid meat; other imaginative dishes (duck breasts in Cassis – blackcurrant liqueur); fine cheese selection; wine: Reserve du Patron only 19F;

Well-preserved market town, on edge of industrial belt, where river Lys and Aire canal meet. 18th-century Grand'Place has many old houses; town hall (16th century) is attractive; 15th-century church of St Peter in Flamboyant-Renaissance style. British Army HQ 1917–18.

Gros Plant 21F. Menu 45–
105F; rooms 50–150F. Shut
Sun. evenings, Mon.; 15
Jan.–15 Feb.

**N43 Béthune
(25km)**

Vieux Beffroy, Grand'Place
(21) 25.15.00: well-run
auberge with good-value
meals; menu 55–80F; rooms
80–150F.

At Noeux-les-Mines, 3km on
D937 – Les Tourterelles (21)
66.90.75: old house; recently
changed from Logis to 2-star
hotel. Recommended to me
by a rival restaurant keeper!
Regional cooking, menu 55–
95F; rooms 90–165F. Shut
Sun. evenings.

Industrial town, rebuilt
considerably after damage in
two world wars, but some
pleasant 17th-century
buildings left. Grand'Place
rebuilt in Flemish style.

D937 Arras **(33km)**	See **Route 4.**

D939 Cambrai
(36km)

At Marquion (11km before Cambrai) – La Crémaillère (21) 22.50.31: cheap and good; old, classic cooking of good ingredients; plus some surprises such as duck stew, cabbage stuffed with scallops; menu 38–48F. Shut Mon.

Cambrai – Rotisserie à l'Escargot, rue de Gaulle (27) 81.24.54: young patron-chef building reputation for value and reliability; menu 50–100F. Shut Mon.; part of Jan. and June.

Aux 17 Provinces, rue Liniers (27) 81.27.68: simple; good value; menu 39F; shut Sun. evening, Mon.

Château de la Motte-Fenelon, square du Château (27) 83.61.38: this early 19th-century château in a park has recently changed hands; new owner much respected in restaurant business but I have not yet revisited it. .

Tank warfare started here: on 20 November 1917, the Tank Corps, 4000 men strong, launched the first tank attack in history, winning a victory and changing the history of war. Linen has been made here since the 15th century. A small town packed with historic and art treasures. Do see the church of Saint Géry, with 85m (250ft) belfry, a Renaissance-style rood screen, and twelve large paintings, including *The Entombment* by Rubens. Fénelon, the churchman, writer and soldier, who got himself badly wounded fighting the Duke of Marlborough, was Archbishop of Cambrai and died there. The massive 14th-century Porte de Paris was part of the old defences. In municipal museum are works of Breughel and Rubens. Handsome covered market.

Pricey, but said to be excellent. Menu 120–180F; grill menu 50F; rooms 143–160F; heated pool; shut Sun. evenings; part August.

N43 Le Cateau (23km)

At Ligny (on D74 off N43 or D16 from Caudry) – Château de Ligny (27) 85.25.84: pricey but very attractive; in lovely 13th-century château; calm, peaceful; deer and ponies wander the park; dine by candlelight in the chimney corner; polite service; superb dishes changed according to season and availability *fresh*. A Relais de Campagne of Châteaux Hôtels de France. Menu 120F lunch; evening à la carte; lovely rooms 280–350F; shut 1 Jan.–1 Feb.

The artist Henri Matisse was born here in 1869 and a museum in the 17th-century town hall contains his drawings and engravings. Also birthplace of Adolphe Mortier, giant son of a cloth merchant, who became one of Napoleon's best marshals. Made Duke of Treviso, he died protecting King Louis Philippe with his great bulk from explosions of an 'infernal machine'.

**N43 La Capelle
(30km)**

At La Villa Pasques, 17 rue de L'Armistice (then rue d'Hirson), the German General von Winderfeld came on 7 November 1918 to meet Marshal Foch's staff to arrange the end of the Kaiser's war. The Haudroy Stone, a mile northeast, commemorates the Armistice of 11 November 1918. Capelle has an important race course.

**N43 Hirson
(14km)**

Restaurant Feutry, Hôtel de la Gare, pl. Gare (23) 58.16.45: new owner for the station hotel; simple place; new reputation for cooking simple dishes well. Six menus: 35–130F; rooms 45–70F. Shut Sun. evenings.

Commercial centre where two rivers meet; superb forest with small lakes right alongside; Etang de Blangy is pretty, with a waterfall. From Etang du Pas Baynard (3 miles from town) is a summer 'Route Verte', open 1 May to 30 September, through the forest. Fine oak trees. Fine views along ridge road from Hirson. Cheese and cider country.

**N43 Mon Idée
D877 to Rocroi,
then local road
D1 to Revin
and right
through valley
of the Meuse.**

Rocroi – Commerce, pl. A. Briand (24) 35.11.15: *another* Hôtel de Commerce which my readers love. Mme Marcelle Copernici deserves their praise for value, Mme Tobie-Copernici, her daughter, for cooking; simple dining room made pleasant by the feminine touch. You won't go hungry; happy atmosphere and service; try cheese tarts, coq au vin, veal kidneys in white wine; nice gâteaux; wild boar in season. Menu 42–80F; rooms 65–140F.

The French Ardennes, a real wanderers' route, sometimes steep, very beautiful and wild and almost totally unknown to tourists. You pass massive dark ravine of Les Dames de Meuse. At the bridge of Roches de Laifur are magnificent views of this ravine and the wild rocky cliffs. Montherme, where the Meuse meets the river Semoy, has a fine old town on the Meuse left bank and a 12th-century fortified church. Then you pass the legendary Roche des Quatre Fils Aymon

– the legend of the horse Bayard who took four brothers to safety when pursued by Charlemagne's troops. It was Bayard who put his hoof down at Hirson to make Etang du Pas Baynard. Amusing to be in country where, against all the propaganda of school history books, Charlemagne was the villain and local heroes fought against him.

In this country, too, the French fought in the 17th century to free Flanders and the Champagne from Spanish Empire. Revin was once Spanish. At Rocroi, the future Prince of Condé defeated Spain in 1643.

Victor Hugo, George Sand and the poet Rimbaud all lived in the Ardennes and wrote of its beauty – spectacular, sometimes dark and sombre. Country of trout, wild boar and deer.

D1 Charleville-Mézières (29km)

On D1 just before Charleville – Auberge de la Fôret (24) 33.37.55: Michel Baudlet once cooked at the London Ritz; good value; menu and plats du jour change daily according to availability of fresh produce. Menu 50–95F; Shut Sun. evenings, Mon.

Town-planned by Charles de Gonzague, a well-connected local duke, in the early 17th century, it has the usual planners' trick whereby all main streets meet at right angles; arcaded place Ducal, town centre, is suitably noble. A pleasant town, on both sides of the river Meuse. In the 1914–18 war, the Kaiser and his son, Little Willie, often lived here. It has been the scene of battle after battle through centuries, but

Charleville-Mézières *continued*

Charleville – Relais du Square, pl. Gare (24) 33.38.76: charming dining room overlooking flower garden, neat, clean, simple, good meat includes boar. Menu 45–68F; rooms 80–160F.

in peacetime it produces those splendid heavy French cooking pans. After its terrible battering in 1918 it was adopted by Manchester whose people helped to rebuild it. A main suburb is called Manchester.

N43 Sedan (23km)

Chariot d'Or, pl. de Torcy (24) 29.04.87: furniture, crockery, and table linen renewed; range of menus from simple weekday at 37F (pork chop or fish, boudin blanc sausage and cheese) to 90F Sunday gastronomic – good (sometimes includes oysters stuffed with almond); splendid smoked boar ham; duck with green peppers; menu 37, 70F weekdays, 50, 90F Sundays; shut Sat.; Fri. eve.; Sun. eve.; all July.

Au Bon Vieux Temps, pl. de la Halle (24) 29.03.70: alas, in a restaurant once highly praised, readers write of surly service, long waits, cold atmosphere. I leave it in for some excellent dishes, such as fritures de Meuse – fried river fish – and lamb with mango fruit; Michelin star; menu 40, 90F; carte around 130F. Shut Sun. eve.; Mon.

Road much nicer since motorway was built parallel. Pretty in places. An industrial town now and a good place to eat, it has played a big part in French history; its castle, biggest in Europe (15th-century) was studied for centuries by military architects from around the world. Became a Protestant stronghold. Scene of last stand against Prussians by Napoleon III's army under General MacMahon. French surrendered here.

N43 Bazeilles, Douzy, Montmédy (44km)

Le Mady, pl. Poincaré (29) 80.10.87: local favourite; own trout tank; hors d'oeuvres buffet; Catalan-style (fish and meat) paella. Menu at 43F includes ¼-bottle of wine; others 48, 80F. Wines from 22F; simple rooms 45–70F; shut Mon.; Feb.

Château of Bazeilles – built by a Sedan draper 1742; elegant and charming Renaissance building. Open Easter–mid Oct. Maison de la Dernière Cartouche (Last Cartridge), where a French marine unit fought incredibly bravely against Germans in

1870. Museum of that Franco-Prussian War, open 1 April–30 Sept. Douzy has lake for sailing, fishing, swimming.

Montmédy citadel was restored by Vauban, the 17th-century military engineer who specialised in conducting sieges, restoring old forts and who invented the socket bayonet.

N43 Longuyon (25km) N381 Briey, Metz (94km)

Le Crinouc, rue Général Metman (87) 74.12.46: young chef Philippe Canonne leans heavily towards the simple Nouvelle Cuisine, but the high apostles of that cult accuse him of using too many sauces and serving dishes 'trop endimanché' (too dressed up for Sunday), which is fine for me! I think he has it right. 5 menus between 80F and 200F. Wines 35–360F. Rooms 145–154F. Shut Sun. evening

Marville is an interesting little town with many old houses with carved façades from the Spanish occupation (16th to 17th centuries).

Longuyon is set in wooded hills where two rivers meet. Scenery on this run is pleasant, with valleys and plains, and is little known to tourists.

Metz, a big commercial centre at the meeting of rivers Moselle and Seille, is extremely pleasant; picturesque islands in the river, a fine old town with narrow streets and old buildings, and a superb Gothic cathedral with a 90m (300ft) tower and fine stained glass. Metz was captured by Germans in 1870, held by them until 1918; they took it again in 1940; it was freed by the Americans in 1944.

Briey, Metz
continued

At Ars-sur-Moselle (10km on D6 SW) – Britons go here for for the postmark on letters home, French and Belgians to eat at – Auberge de la Gare (87) 60.62.63: happy atmosphere, good service; good Alsatian cooking, classic style with cream sauces; no Nouvelle here; try sucking pig (cochon de lait en gêlée), trout in Riesling; good Alsace wines, interesting Lorraine 'gris'. Menu 75–165F.

N3 to St Avold
N56 Sarralbe
N61, N4 to
Saverne
(131km)

St Avold – L'Europe, rue Altmayer (87) 92.00.33: modern Logis, modern furnishings; pleasant bedrooms with bathrooms; garden. Menu 36–120F; (shut Sat.); rooms 150–210F.

Saverne – Chez Jean, rue Gare (88) 91.10.19: in typical Alsatian building; good Alsatian cooking by la Patronne's son, and Alsatian wine; salmon soufflé with lobster sauce, sauerkraut dishes, good trout in Riesling, succulent steak; menu 40–120F; rooms 68–123F. Shut 1–10 Sept.; 1–18 Jan.

Geiswiller, rue de la Côte (88) 91.18.51: excellent local cooking at moderate prices, and dearer gastronomic dishes. Menu 45–140F; rooms 75–155F. Shut Mon. out of season.

St Avold is on the edge of the coalfields, but this beautiful hilly road across the Lorraine plains is pleasantly wooded in stretches and has fine hilltop views. You cross the river Saar at Sarralbe then after Phalsbourg run up Col de Saverne, then downhill with more good long views. The Col has botanic gardens.

Saverne: in a rocky valley at the foot of the Vosges mountains, where the river Zorn meets the Marne–Rhine canal; well worth a little time. Château des Rohans, built by the dissolute Cardinal de Rohan in the 18th century as cardinal-bishops' residence, is a grandiose, classic building in rose pink – this area is famous for its roses. It faces the canal, in a park where a *son et lumière* is held on three summer evenings a week from June to August. Many old buildings, including two in wood next to town hall.

Château du Haut-Barr (5km by D102, D171): romantic castle ruins; superb views; built 12th century; once HQ of a secret Alsace wine-drinking brotherhood. Member who gave away admission secrets lost his sense of taste and smell for wine for 2 years!

N4 to Marmoutier and Wasselonne then Strasbourg (39km)

At Marlenheim on N4, 20km before Strasbourg – Hostellerie Reeb, rue Schweitzer (88) 87.52.70: excellent modern hotel with beautifully furnished air-conditioned bedrooms, all with own bath or shower, wc; gastronomic restaurant; grill room with open wood fire; menu 45–180F; wines 25–150F; rooms 130F (excellent value); shut Thurs., Jan.

Strasbourg – apart from its foie gras pâté, Strasbourg is one of the great gourmet cities of Europe and seven restaurants are starred by Michelin. These are pricey, of

Between Saverne and Strasbourg is the beautiful Dabo-Wagenbourg country, separating Alsace and Lorraine. Marmoutier has a spectacular Romanesque church with crowded towers. Wasselonne is an ancient fortified city among pleasant hills. The run into Strasbourg is between hop gardens and vineyards. Though one of France's biggest cities, Strasbourg has charm, being on the banks of the Rhine where it meets the river Ill and the Rhone and Marne canals. Cathedral in red sandstone was started in 1176, on the foundations of

Strasbourg
continued

course. But there are also some excellent little restaurants which are much cheaper and good value in their own range.

Buffet de la Gare, pl. Gare (88) 32.68.28: the first-floor room serves a good 39F menu and other menus up to 110F including delicious foie gras, pâté en croûte, steak with pepper.

La Chaumière, rue Fonderie (88) 32.35.23: classic meat and fish dishes; pot au feu; fish soup; foie gras; menu 50–65F; shut Sun.; Aug.

Maison Kammerzell, pl. Cathédral (88) 32.42.14: a Michelin star for this restaurant on four floors of a remarkable and beautiful Alsatian house; must be for that formidable sauerkraut dish it serves! Ground-floor wine 'stube' now called Léo Schnug, with menus at 85F and 105F with drinks; other floors 125–175F. Huge choice of menus and dishes includes Nouvelle Cuisine on first floor – cannot be for the locals, must be for EEC members and civil servants. Shut Fri.

At Lampertheim, 10km on D64 – Hostellerie de Lampertheim, rue d'Eglise (88) 20.13.58: renovated, excellent value meals 38–55F; rooms 130–150F.

an earlier church, and completed in 1439. You climb 525 steps up the spire 150m (472ft) high to see town and country beyond. Splendid museum (L'Oeuvre Notre-Dame), a collection of ancient houses with wood galleries and containing sculptures from cathedral.

Also the Château des Rohans, built for the cardinals, houses three museums and has magnificent rooms; in its beaux-arts departments are masterpieces by Rubens, El Greco, Rembrandt, Van Dyck, Van Goyen, Fragonard, Sisley, Renoir and Corot. Older narrow streets have timbered houses; medieval bridges over Ill river. European Parliament building has a fine old garden opposite.

Route 6 Cherbourg to Hendaye

(for Spain and Portugal)

A route of discovery, to find new places to revisit and explore more thoroughly, like the little seaside resorts of the Cotentin peninsula below Cherbourg, south Normandy and southeast Brittany, the waterways of the almost secretive Marais Poitevin, and the huge sand beaches with Atlantic rollers of Les Landes, backed by vast forests planted in the 18th century to stop blowing sand and soil erosion.

You can save time by cutting corners, especially at the beginning, but this peninsula deserves time for discovery.

We have deliberately missed Bordeaux, though it is a fine place to eat. Traffic can be fierce and the wine comes from the villages. Don't miss St Emilion. The N10 road is best avoided where possible. It is difficult to decide whether to explore the Marais or divert west for La Rochelle – beautiful old houses, historically interesting, fishing harbour with fine fish restaurants, and boats to the big beaches of the Ile de Ré. But Rochelle deserves a week's stay – not an hour or two.

This route is shorter than most usual routes to northwest Spain, and could even be quicker in the high season when the N10 is jammed. From St Malo, join at Fougères; from other ferry ports, join at Avranches.

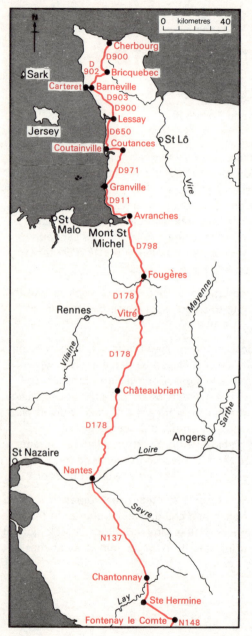

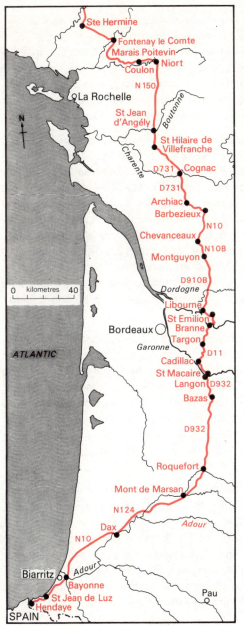

Ste Hermine

Fontenay le Comte
Marais Poitevin
Coulon   Niort

N 150

La Rochelle

St Jean
d'Angély

St Hilaire de
Villefranche

D731   Cognac

D731

Archiac
Barbezieux
                N10
Chevanceaux
                N10B
Montguyon

D910B
Dordogne
Libourne
St Emilion
Branne
Targon
Garonne
Bordeaux
                D11
Cadillac
St Macaire
Langon D932
Bazas

D932

Roquefort

Mont de Marsan

N124
Adour
Dax
N10

Adour
Biarritz
Bayonne   Pau
St Jean de Luz
Hendaye
SPAIN

ATLANTIC

N

0 kilometres 40

Boutonne

Charente

Cherbourg   • PARIS

Hendaye

From rich Norman dishes you pass to oysters of Brittany, for Cancale is across the bay from the Granville –Avranches coast, and Le Croisic, nursery of Portugaise oysters, is in the Loire estuary near Nantes. The land between is rich in lamb, veal and river fish. Breton crêpes (creamy omelettes) are eaten locally at 5pm with cider – a snack between lunch and dinner.

Poitou-Charentes, between Nantes and Bordeaux, has some of the most fertile land and productive water of France; rich dairy and beef pastures, salt-washed sheep pastures, a huge variety of vegetables and fruit, including Charentais melons, oyster beds and mussel farms; and the La Rochelle fishing fleet bringing in a variety of fish. Cooking is in butter, with liberal doses of cream and wine, and dishes are lighter than in Bordeaux. Oysters are served with little spicy sausages, mussels in creamy liquid (called mouclade); moules bordelaises are mussels in wine and tomato sauce.

True Bordelaise sauce is made with claret, not rough plonk, and butter, tomatoes, beef marrow, shallots, thyme and nutmeg. It goes best with beef, which goes best with Bordeaux wine. Superb Adour river salmon from Les Landes, south of Bordeaux, is cooked in red wine and sauce. Here they often cook in goose fat; game is plentiful in the forests. Goose, duck and pork are served fresh and preserved, but vegetables are poor.

A wine of the Nantes area, Gros Plant, is akin to Muscadet but with an acidity which most French like. In such short space, there is little to say about wines of Bordeaux except: 'Drink them!' But a good tip for money-saving, if you find the great Médoc wines too dear (Pavilac, Margaux, St Estéphe), is to buy Côtes de Blayes, and Bourg wines from across the Dordogne river – they are reliable, enjoyable and cheap.

Route 6 Cherbourg to Hendaye

(for Spain and Portugal)

Le Vauban, quai Caligny (33) 53.12.29: locals as well as hordes of British flock to Claude Deniau's two-faced restaurant – to the 'snack' for a 50F meal with superb help-yourself hors d'oeuvres and the dearer à la carte restaurant for dishes of Normandy: ham in cider, Boudin brochet, civet of lobster, scallops in cider, various crêpe flambé in Calvados, the apple spirit; huge platter of seafood would make a meal. Prices high, wines rather dear. Frankly I would stick to the 'snack'. Shut Fri., Feb.

Pleasant port with attractive harbour, sandy beach. Market – fruit, vegetables, flowers, some clothes – in place de Gaulle Tues., Thurs., Sat. mornings; pavement cafés in this square; small shops in small streets off it. Continent Hypermarket Quai de l'Entrepôt, near harbour. In J. F. Millet museum, works of Millet, peasant who painted country scenes so truly (he lived later in Jersey); also Flemish school paintings including Van Eyck, Van Dyck and Rembrandt, and a Botticelli. Fish market

Cherbourg
continued

Le Cotentin, quai Caligny (33) 53.56.22: brasserie ideal for quick first/last meals; restaurant above; menu 40, 60, 100F. Can be noisy.

off rue au Blé. In Hitler's war, retreating Germans blew up harbour, but British frogmen cleared debris and mines and it became main Allied supply port, handling twice New York's 1939 capacity. Pluto, Allied underground oil pipeline, ran here from Isle of Wight.

West 5km at Nacqueville is a fine château in a lovely setting of wooded hills and a river. At Gruchy on N coast is the house where Millet was born.

D3, then soon on to D900 Bricquebec (20km)

Vieux Château (33) 52.24.49: sometimes you wish you had kept something to yourself! I found Hubert Hardy's delightful hotel in part of the castle when he moved in 7 years ago and thought he deserved publicity. Now it pays to book ahead! Prices remain very reasonable. Prettily furnished bedrooms vary much in size; Queen Victoria slept in the biggest, of course. Lovely fish, nice local lamb; good straightforward cooking.

Most interesting little place with a 14th-century castle. Queen Victoria stayed here in 1857 after visiting Cherbourg for the opening of the railway to Caen. Climb 160 steps up the keep for fine views of countryside and the Trappist monastery (Abbaye Notre-Dame-de-Grâce) 3km along D121. Market before castle gates on Mondays.

Wines reasonable (from 25F); menu 35, 55, 80F; rooms 85–160F; shut Jan. Worth driving from Cherbourg for a first meal.

Henry V gave the castle to the Duke of Suffolk after Agincourt, but he gave it back to the French later as part of his ransom.

D902
Barneville-
Carteret (20km)

Marine, Carteret (33) 54.83.31: I dared to recommend it to one of Europe's leading restaurant owners – and he approved heartily; outstanding fish and shellfish straight from the harbour; really nice moules marinières; turbot, sole, brill – whatever the fishermen catch. Locals and holidaymakers use it; large dining room, mock beams, sea views; menu 55–89F; house-wine 23F (red, white, rosé); rooms 76–184F.

Les Isles, Barneville (33) 54.90.76: facing fine sand beach; seaview on the menu painted by Marie Duplaissy, wife of patron and spare-time artist; splendid old-fashioned cooking in butter; try quiche aux moules (mussel flan); caneton vallée d'Auge (duck in cream, cider, Calvados with mushrooms); shellfish platter; local lamb 'pré-salé' (from salt-marshes, like Romney Marsh lamb); menu 60–90F; rooms 90–200F. Shut 15 Nov.–20 Dec.

Twin family resorts, with Carteret the lively bit, Barneville with bigger beach. Plenty to amuse children. The estuary harbour – nearest harbour to Jersey – is constantly interesting, with a genuine fishing fleet and the catch sold on the harbourside; yachts coming in from Britain and the Channel Isles, fish being packed, nets drying. A nice small beach and a large sand beach reached across dunes or by a lovely cornice walk over the headland (Customs Officers' Path) with changing views (about 25 mins). Barneville has an 11th-century church with fine painted Romanesque arches inside. Monument to the cutting of Cotentin peninsula by American forces prior to the capture of Cherbourg in 1944.

D903 then
D900 to Lessay
(29km)

Hostellerie de l'Abbaye (33) 46.43.88: pleasant, quiet, well-run; good meals; strong, garlicky fish soup; menu 50F and à la carte; rooms 80–160F; shut Nov.; Mondays. Recommended to

A pleasant little town among windy moorland, it has an abbey founded in 1056 by William the Conqueror's family and which is a masterpiece of Norman architecture; it was almost

Lessay
continued

me by Douglas Barrington of Lygon Arms, Broadway – doyen of British hotel-keepers.

Normandie (33) 46.41.11: Relais Routiers and 1-star hotel; simple, cheap; excellent food. Menu 30–40F; rooms 50–70F.

Between La Haye du Puits and Lessay, near Angoville-sur-Ay – La Campagnelle (33) 46.01.92: lively 'fun' restaurant open in season from lunchtime until 11.30pm. Nice garden for summer lunch; music at night; bar made from old farmcart; gimmicky but good value; menu 50F; wines from 25F; closed mid Sept.–mid Oct.

destroyed in the invasion fighting of 1944 but has been carefully and beautifully restored, using original stone and old tools. Benedictines from abbey started Fair of Sainte-Croix, still held mid September – one of the biggest in Normandy. Vast quantities of sausages, beef and lamb spitroast to be eaten with cider; lovely colts and pied cattle sold in hundreds. Tents and funfair cover the moor.

If you prefer horses to the sea, you can now take D900 to the St-Lô French national stud with 250 stallions (mostly English and Norman), though most are only there mid July to mid February. Visits 10–11.30; 14.30–17hrs. Then take D999 past Mount Robin (only 995 feet high but good view) and D972 to rejoin route at Coutances.

D650
Coutainville
(20km)

Hardy (33) 47.04.11: Oh, dear! What do I report? I have sent dozens by recommendation, hundreds through my writing, to this simple family hotel in the same family for three generations and until recently all were delighted – not so much for chintzy bedrooms as for Emile Hardy's superb cuisine, known in many countries. Now, suddenly, some readers complain of offhand service, disorganisation

Little coast road passing a series of seaside villages with beaches almost totally unknown to Britons. (Alternative is D2, D68, D272 inland.) Coutainville is a fin-de-siècle resort where you expect to see starch-uniformed nannies pushing high prams along the promenade. Still some genuine old bathing huts on the big sand beach; sand dunes; little shops. A friendly place where you can get to know French families.

(especially during redecoration). So I sent a spy (another travel writer) who returned raving about the cooking. Some bedrooms *are* small and crowded. Menu 58–180F; wines from 25F; rooms 115–130F. Shut Mon. off-season; Jan.

Neptune, on promenade (33) 47.07.66: nice white fin-de-siècle hotel beside beach; comfortable; no restaurant; rooms 133–183F. Shut Nov., Dec., Jan.

D44 Coutances (13km)

Relais du Viaduc, ave Verdun (33) 45.02.68: unassuming, delightful inn with covered pavement terrace, like a set for a French film; Logis de France and Relais Routiers; patron-chef Marcel Hossin is a very good cook. Nice Norman dishes – turkey sauté with leaks, sole Dieppoise (poached in wine with mussels and shrimps; mushroom and cream sauce); nice desserts; menu 28–90F (28F real filling Routiers meal); rooms 60–110F. Shut 10 Sept.–10 Oct.

Au P'tit Home, rue d'Harcourt (33) 45.00.67: little corner restaurant, pleasant inside; local dishes nicely cooked; good shellfish and sole Normande: desserts with a crème Chantilly base; menu 35, 48, 65, 90F; good wine choice, plus local cider; shut Monday; 12 Sept.–12 Oct.

A lovely little town on a hilltop crowned by a really beautiful cathedral, much rebuilt in the 13th century but originally 11th century, mostly built by the incredible de Hauteville family who went to Italy and became Norman kings of large areas; the famous King Roger of Sicily was one of them. From one tower you can often see Jersey. Fifteen cathedral windows are 13th century; oldest show St George, St Thomas (à Becket) of Canterbury and St Blaise.

Coutances
continued

At Montpinchon, 13km on D7, D27 – Château de la Salle (33) 46.95.19: expensive but beautiful; Relais de Campagne of Châteaux Hôtels; L-shaped low-built manor house; superbly furnished; lovely dining room; menu 130–200F; wines 45–350F; rooms 290–350F; shut 1 Nov.–26 March.

The public flower gardens are beautiful, with magnificent cedar trees; the gardens are illuminated on weekends (1 July to 15 September).

D971 Granville (29km)

At Trelly, left at Quettreville (10km from Coutances) – Verte Campagne (33) 47.65.33: by request of dozens of readers – old stone farmhouse with appropriate antique furniture; log fire; pleasant bedrooms, with own bathrooms; cooking praised

Our Victorian ancestors loved it. Nicely protected by rocks, it can be a suntrap. Roc-Point, joined to mainland by a rocky isthmus, was once an English fort (15th century). If you have no time to explore the historic old town and ramparts, go up to the

by an expert; good value; menu 55–90F; rooms 60–200F; restaurant shut Mondays.

Granville – Normandie-Chaumière, rue Paul-Poirier (33) 50.01.71: pretty; thatched roof and courtyard where you can eat in nice weather; excellent fish, shellfish; escalope Normande (with cream, Calvados and apple); menu 45–105F; rooms 58–120F. Shut Wed. except July, Aug.; Tues. evening in winter.

unpronounceable place de l'Isthme for superb views to Brittany. Narrow beach; best beaches at Donville (15 mins by cliff path) and St Pair au Mer (3km along D911) – golden sands safe for children. Granville museum has fine collection of folk head-dresses. For centuries, Granville was a big fishing port. In Elizabethan days – 16th century – its ships fished for cod off Newfoundland. Now the industry is dead.

D911 along coast to Avranches (33km)

St Jean-le-Thomas – Les Bains (33) 48.84.20: over many years readers have sent much praise for André Gautier's 2-star Logis. It has added a heated swimming pool and a beachside annexe to cope with high-season visitors. M. Gautier's Norman cooking is the biggest pull – outstanding scallops; mussels in cider; sole; sauté chicken in cider on a bed of cream; or, by order, lobster flambé in Calvados; menu 42–110F; wines from 25F; rooms 59–150F. Shut 10 Oct.–March.

La Plage (33) 48.84.17: recommended to me as alternative when Les Bains is closed or full; known for big portions of well-cooked dishes; guinea fowl; coq au vin; local fish; menu 35 (weekday), 60, 110F; garden tables for summer; rooms 50–60F; shut Fri. off-season; Jan.

This coast road is well worth a diversion for small beach resorts pleasant for future holidays or weekends away: Jullouville (rather exclusive resort with fine sands backed by pine trees); St-Jean-le-Thomas (pleasant village looking across sandbanks to Mont-St-Michel). Gen. Eisenhower, wartime Allied C-in-C, was so impressed he mentioned the view in his war memoirs. Rich in mimosa and wisteria in season.

Avranches, a charming town, is deeply involved in Anglo-French history; here Henry II of England knelt and received absolution from the Pope because his foolhardy knights had murdered Thomas à Becket; you can still see the stone (La Plate-forme) on which he knelt. From here General 'Blood and Guts' Patton and his

Avranches
continued

Avranches – La Croix d'Or, rue Constitution (33) 58.04.88: pretty Norman building; old furniture, leather in dining room; regional cooking; try crayfish in cream; dodine de canard (boned, stuffed duck, like ballatine); menu 60–180F; rooms 50–200F. Shut Jan.

newly formed Third Army of the US Forces launched on 1 August 1944 their first attack against the Nazis which took them right across Europe. The Patton memorial here has an inscription: 'Making the Avranches breakthrough in the roar of its tanks, while marching towards victory and the liberation of France, the glorious American Army of General Patton passed over this crossroads.' The British and Commonwealth memorial at Bayeux is more succinct: 'We whom William conquered have freed the land of the Conqueror.'

Here too in 1639 the French peasants under Jean Quetil (Jean Nu-Pieds – John Barefoot) started a less successful revolt which had repercussions right up to the French Revolution.

D798 Fougères (40km)

Les Voyageurs, pl. Gambetta (99) 99.14.17: good reputation for food; try turbot pâté en croute, pleasant service; menu 50–100F; wines from 22F; rooms 90–160F.

Industrial town now, but historically interesting. The English captured the castle several times (1166–1499); its shell remains, surrounding a park, on a rock above a loop in the river; walk along the ramparts past the old towers, climb Tour Mélusine for a fine view of the town, cross the river Nançon to a public garden, place aux Arbres, made in terraces from old ramparts. 14th-century church of St Sulpice has amusing gargoyles. Shoes are made here, and a castle museum shows footwear through the ages.

D178 Vitré (29km)

Chêne Vert, pl. Gare (99) 75.00.58: very popular; book ahead high season; huge choice; menu 35 (weekday), 48, 70F; 200 different wines; rooms 45–130F. Shut Sat.; 9 Sept.–9 Oct.

Petit Billot, pl. Gen-Leclerc (99) 75.02.10: big portions, good choice; menu 45, 72F (good value); rooms 60–150F. Shut Fri. eve.; Sat. lunch off-season; 15 Dec.–15 Jan.

Lovely view of town as you enter on D178. Then you step into the Middle Ages in a charming town of narrow streets and medieval houses, many of timber. Vitré Castle is triangular with big corner towers and town walls attached; splendidly grotesque carvings; drawbridge. Another medieval castle – Château des Rochers – on a hill 7km south on D88. Madame de Sévigné, beautiful, witty and bitchy chronicler of French 17th-century life, lived there when not in Paris. Vitré was staunchly Protestant, and the 15th-century Notre-Dame Church has an external pulpit from which preachers harangued the Calvinists.

D178 Châteaubriant (50km)

Hostellerie de la Ferrière, route de Nantes (40) 28.00.28: old turreted creeper-clad manor with pleasant gardens, lawns; Louis XV-style dining room; friendly, family atmosphere; local dishes; good fish; speciality ris de veau au whisky (sweet breads in whisky); local cider; menu 48, 53, 90F; rooms 165–190F.

A sad history to this old fortified town: in the castle which still stands the beautiful Françoise Laval, mistress of King Francis I, was imprisoned by her husband, in a room hung with black, until her death. On 20 October 1941 the Nazis shot twenty-seven local people in a sandpit as a reprisal against French Resistance – the first of their mass executions in France. A memorial marks the spot at La Sablière.

**D178 Nantes
(70km)**

At Moisden la Rivière (12km along D178) – La Chaumière (40) 81.61.23: village inn; good value; country cooking; bargain wine list – Muscadet 26F; house-wine 20F; Provence rosé 25F; Beaujolais 32F; St Emilion '75, 78F; menu 27.50–52F (lunch); 30–50F (evening). Shut 1–22 Aug.

In Nantes, many good restaurants cater for expense-account trade, with high prices. Even my old favourite bargain spot Chez Biret is renamed and gone a bit upmarket. Now called: Le Nantais, rue Hauts-Pavés (40) 76.59.54: regional and solid bourgeoise cooking; good shellfish, excellent white fish in a beurre Nantais (butter whipped with shallots and Muscadet); menu 65–98F; lunch only except dinner also Fri., Sat.; shut first 3 weeks Aug.

Restaurant du Change, rue Juiverie (40) 48.02.28: in old quarter; country décor; patron-chef; strong on fish; menu 40F (weekdays), 60, 105F; shut mid July–mid Aug.

Le Coq Hardi, allée Cdt-Charcot (40) 74.14.25: attractive; good service; value; menu 50–85F; shut Sat.; July.

At Les Sorinières (12km on D178) – Abbaye de Villeneuve (40) 04.40.25: expensive but delightful and

For men only – near La Meilleraye, 12km from Châteaubriant, is a Trappist abbey with a restored 12th-century church. Only men may enter. It is beside a big pool. Nantes, on the Breton side of the Loire, is not truly Breton today and is not pretty – an industrial centre, but with very great historic interest and some hidden treasures: Ducal castle (mostly 15th-century) where the Edict of Nantes was issued in 1598 giving many political rights and religious freedoms to Protestants. Anne of Brittany was mainly responsible for its building. Best part is the Renaissance Tour de la Couronne d'Or, with fine Italian-inspired loggias. Museum of Popular Art has absorbing collections from Breton culture and life – from head-dresses to furniture, including interesting cooking equipment. Fine Arts Museum (rue Gambetta) contains a big collection of paintings from primitives to moderns, including some fine Rubens'. Cathedral is more interesting than it looks from outside. The covered way, with shops, steps and statues, Passage Pommeraye, is a lovable piece of ostentation. Pleasant Jardin des Plantes has a statue of Jules Verne (born here). Pleasant trips by boat on river Erdre (from ¾-hour).

beautiful décor; elegant bedrooms; in peaceful park with swimming pool; 18th-century house; Relais de Campagne; splendid service; excellent imaginative cooking (salmon with chicory braised in beer); good desserts; menu 120–200F; rooms 300–350F.

N137 to Chantonnay (73km) Ste Hermine (17km) then N148 to Fontenay-le-Comte (total 112km)

Old town of Fontenay straddles the Vendée river; near place Viete, the centre, is the old part, with 16th- to 17th-century houses. Town hall is on the site of the convent where Rabelais was educated. Château de Terre-Neuve, built for the poet Rapin in the 16th century, has Renaissance statues, chimneypieces and mantels, and fine views from the terrace. Worth seeing.

Local roads D938, D68 to Abbey of Maillezais, then local roads south and east along Sèvre river to Coulon (40km)

Coulon – Au Marais, quai Louis Tardy (49) 25.90.43: place to try local dishes, such as mouclade Maraichine (local mussels in cream and wine), bouilliture d'anguilles (small eels stewed in white wine with onions and eggs), crayfish; fish terrine; nice local gâteau; great wild game; menu 48–87F; rooms 132F. Try also Pineau, Charente's mixture of brandy and grape juice which can be drunk with shellfish, as an apéritif, or, says the publicity, 'at tea time'. Restaurant (not hotel) shut mid Dec.–mid Jan.

Marais Poitevin – marshes drained in the 11th to 16th centuries to make a delightful 'Green Venice' of waterways among trees and peaceful little villages where people still live as much by freshwater fishing for carp, perch, crayfish and tiny eels (anguilles) as dairy farming with cows and goats. Flat-bottomed boats (*plattes*) propelled by poles still used for moving stock and taking people shopping, to church and to school. Strange, little-known area. Coulon Church, in main square, dates back to Charlemagne. Take a *platte*

Coulon
continued

from here for a peaceful water trip, under arches of trees, to see other villages.

Abbey of Maillezais, built in the 10th century, has a ruined church, 14th-century abbey buildings and parish church with a superb Romanesque façade. Rabelais spent some time here, and in Religious Wars the abbey was fortified as a Protestant stronghold.

D9 (local) Niort (11km)

Hôtel Terminus, Restaurant Poelle d'Or, rue Gare (49) 24.00.38: chef-patron Jean Louis Tavernier has handed over the cooking in his very popular restaurant to his assistant of 15 years, Robert Frittoli. Still serves fricassé of Marais eels; sole in Muscadet; but terrine of duck is now in Pineau! All very good but I shall miss M. Tavernier's touches as 'High Master of the Fine Throats in Poitou'. He still runs the show, but travels abroad as

Riverside town rich in flowers in season, and with tiny green islands where the river flows into channels. Two enormous towers and ramparts left from the castle built by Henry II of England, completed by Richard Lionheart, now a museum of Poitou costumes. Good open-air swimming pool and an ice rink. Renaissance former town hall, now museum, was originally Chaumont Mansion where Madame de Maintenon,

ambassador of French cuisine. Bedrooms completely restored; 43 rooms with bath, shower, toilets; also has a snack bar open mid-day–11pm. Menu 45–120F; rooms 58–160F. Restaurant shut Sat.

Motel des Rocs, Chavagne (11km by D5) (49) 25.50.38: France Accueil hotel; modern, attractive, comfortable; bedrooms wc, bath; meals 60–125F; rooms 165F.

At St Remy (6km on N148) – Relais du Poitou (49) 73.43.99: M. Gaillard's friendly, modern little hotel has good value meals, reasonably priced bedrooms; try mouclade; turbot Tahitienne; lamb sauté; country ham; frogs' legs; snails; mogettes (local beans in herbs and cream); menu 52–100F; rooms 80–135F. Rest. shut Mon.

formidable mistress, then wife of Louis XIV was born. Market halls lively and interesting.

N150 St Jean-d'Angély (50km)

11km down N138, at Tout y Faut, well worth taking a diversion on D115 of 7km each way to Dampierre to see the Château of Dampierre-sur-Boutonne; on an island of the river in a lovely valley; an exquisite piece of Renaissance design. From the courtyard see the superb carved friezes; inside are fine Flemish tapestries. St Jean is an old town with narrow streets and old wooden houses on bank of river Boutonne; beautiful

**St Jean-
d'Angély**
continued

Renaissance fountain (1546)
with unhappy name of Pilori
as the pillory once stood
here. Among explorers' and
archaeological items in the
museum is the Citroën
which was the first car to
cross the Sahara, in 1922 –
called 'Golden Cross'.

**N150 to St
Hilaire-de-
Villefranche
(11km) then
D731 Cognac
(36km)**

At St Laurent de Cognac
(6km from Cognac on D732)
– Logis de Beaulieu, Rest.
Alambic (45) 82.30.50:
excellent value; peaceful; in
parkland; fine views of
vineyards; comfortable
rooms, all with bath or
shower; good classic
cooking; famous, exceptional
wine cellar, wines from 27F;
remarkable collection of
cognacs; menu 56–132F;
rooms 75–250F; shut 15
Dec.–1 Jan.

Cognac: many of its
buildings have gone black –
in a good cause; the vapours
from making brandy cover
them with a very tiny fungus
growth! So it is not a
handsome town, despite a
fine new town hall with
charming gardens.
Overlooking the Charente
river is the Château de
Valois where Francis I was
born (the one who met Henry
VIII at the Field of the Cloth
of Gold). He lived here for
some time. Now reduced in
size, it has cellars and guard
room where English
prisoners taken in Canada in
the Seven Years' War were
imprisoned and scratched
drawings on the walls –
cellars now used for
maturing Otard brandy. You
can visit them at set times –
also Hennessy, Martel
cellars. Town museum has
two floors devoted to brandy,
fine paintings of the Flemish
school. Brandy was invented
when Cognac and area
decided that the wine they
sent to England and Holland
should be distilled; officially,
this was to protect the wine
in travelling; the real reason
was to save increasing

freight charges (instant wine – just add water!). The Dutch called it Brandewijn (Burnt Wine), hence 'Brandy'.

D731 to Archiac (20km) D731 to Barbezieux (33km)

Barbezieux – Boule d'Or, boulevard Gambetta (45) 78.22.72: a surprise so near the dreaded N10, 'calme et reposant' – peaceful and relaxing; pretty shaded garden for fine-weather eating; bedrooms all different, mostly frilly and feminine; good cooking with choice of low-priced menus or gastronomic dishes – sole stuffed with foie gras; lovely mussel soup; oysters gratinées; nice pot-roast chicken; 89F menu is remarkable value; good varied wine list; menu 37, 69, 89, 168F; rooms 63–111F. Open all year.

Barbezieux, on the dreaded N10, crammed in summer and dreary, but the town remains bright and cheerful, possibly because it is the capital of Cognac brandy's Petite Champagne. Only this area and La Grande Champagne, a small area nearer to Cognac, may call their brandy Fine Champagne; also produces excellent chickens, marrons glacés and fruits confits (preserved chestnuts and fruit). The 15th-century château is used as a theatre and museum.

N10 Chevenceaux (20km) N10B to Montguyon (11km) D910B to Libourne (54km)

Montguyon – La Poste (46) 04.19.39: smallish, reasonably priced Logis with cheap meals; menu 32–60F includes wine; rooms 60–80F. Recommended by Logis for regional cooking.

Libourne – Hôtel Loubat, rue Chanzy (56) 51.17.58: charming house, beautifully kept; terrace; restaurant called Le Trois Toques; regional dishes; excellent duck, salmon; menu 75–

Libourne was founded by a Kentish knight, Roger of Leybourne, who had been on a crusade with Henry III's son. In Leybourne Church, Kent, is a window showing the gate-tower at Libourne and the castle of Leybourne. From the time when the English were here in the 100 Years' War, Libourne, at this point where the Dordogne meets the river Isle, has been the big port for the export of

Libourne
continued

180F; 250 wines; attached restaurant Le Landais, rue des Treilles, has pleasant garden for fair-weather eating; very good value; try coq au vin; confit of duck; menu 25–64F; wine 20F a litre; also wine merchants of Bordeaux wines. Rooms 90–222F.

wine; the wine was brought down the rivers on *gabares* (flat-bottomed boats) which were broken up at Libourne to make wine casks. There was fierce competition each year to see who could get wine to England first – Libourne or Bordeaux. It is still a market centre for wines of its own area – St Emilion, Pomerol and Fronsac.

Local D17 from near Libourne railway station to St Emilion (6.5km)

Hostellerie de Plaisance, pl. du Clocher (57) 24.72.32: years ago, when a great meal cost 20F, I sat on the terrace of this hostelry looking at the Dordogne valley after a truly good meal, drinking my second bottle of St Emilion with my cheese. This, I decided, was the way I would spend my last hours on earth. The scene is still as beautiful, the food as good, the wine better, alas, for a meal like that the price is now 130F. New chef-patron and I have not yet tried his cooking, but first reports are good, especially of the fricassé of farmyard chicken in St Emilion, mussel soup, duck; menu 78, 130, 170F. Rooms rather pricey 200–270F.

Logis de la Cadène, pl. Marché-au-Bois (56) 24.71.40: lunch only, but excellent value; delightful 18th-century house; chef-patron Françoise Mouliérac here since 1953, still offers pleasant meals and keeps prices down; try confit of

One of the most delightful little towns in France. Built on two hills with views across rooftops to the valley of the Dordogne, it has little houses packed together in steep streets – mostly old, with their own wine cellars and built of yellowy stone which shines gold in the sunlight. The marketplace with an old acacia tree called the Tree of Liberty is calm and almost deserted until market days, when it is crowded and fun. Once fortified, St Emilion still has its ramparts and its old tower left from the days of Henry III, Plantagenet King of England who founded the castle. St Emilion's own 7th-century hermitage is hewn from the rock, complete with bed, table and fountain to make a bathtub. A huge underground shrine nearby, like a ballroom, was hacked out of rock by monks. The atmosphere of the place holds you – helped, of course, by splendid wine. Cheval Blanc, which is red,

duck; river lampreys; chicken 'crapaudine' (split down middle and grilled); menu 30, 40, 55, 70F. Remarkably cheap St Emilion wines; family owns Château La Clotte, grand-cru classé, and sells it at table for same price as from château cellars, 45–60F a bottle. Shut 15–30 June; 1–15 Sept.

rates almost with Lafite and Latour some years, and is strong and robust.

Take D122 towards Castillon, but turn right and right again to Branne, then D11 through Targon to Cadillac (about 45km)

Cadillac – Relais Chez Georges, pl. René-Gérard (56) 27.11.12: remarkable value; good, cheap meals include wine; rooms; shut Sun.; 1–15 Aug.

Château Cadillac is one of the most beautiful châteaux in France; built in 1598 by the colourful Duke d'Epernon who served Henry III, then Henry IV (the Protestant Henry of Navarre) as Governor of Guyenne, colonel-general of French Infantry and Admiral of France; when Henry IV turned Catholic for political reasons, the Duke remained Protestant. So Henry persuaded him to build this castle to distract him from raising troops and making war on the King. It worked; he went on serving Louis XIII after Henry's assassination. It became a prison after the Revolution, but was taken over by local wine interests and opened to the public in 1952. Among its treasures are magnificent carved chimney pieces and superb tapestries. The family chapel is still there, but its bronze monument is in the Louvre. Cadillac wine rates Première Côte de Bordeaux.

D10 to St Macaire and Langon (13km)

At Verdelais (6km N of Langon) – Hostellerie Saint Pierre (56) 63.23.09: good straightforward French cooking; Bordelaise dishes plus a real goose-confit cassoulet draw people from Bordeaux to this country inn; menu 50–120F; wines excellent value from 20F; Sauternes for 55F; rooms 60–90F. Shut Mon. except summer.

Langon – Claude Darroze, cours Gén.-Leclerc (56) 63.00.48: your chance to try a 2-star Michelin meal. Claude Darroze's cooking deserves the stars; a nice balance between classic and his own dishes; light touch without making you feel that you are slimming! One of my favourite cooks. Pricey, of course; menu 100, 175F. Rooms 70–180F.

Langon, a wine market town on the Garonne, is joined by a bridge to St Macaire, a medieval town with ramparts and fortified bridge. Sauterne, the small area producing greatest of sweet wines, starts here. Try it as 'elevenses', not as a dessert wine when you are too replete to really enjoy it. And if any wine experts sound horrified, tell them that the idea came from a very famous mayor of Bordeaux.

A vineyard at St Macaire, Malrome, and its château, was bought by the artist Toulouse-Lautrec's mother. She hoped that here he would regain his health. In 1901 he died here and is buried in the churchyard at Verdelais, 6km north.

D932 Bazas (12km) Roquefort, then Mont-de-Marsan (74km)

Roquefort (*not* the cheese Roquefort) – Le Commerce, rue Thiers (58) 58.50.13: the place to taste the famous local duck (pâté, liver, confit, roast and pot-roast); good roast guinea fowl flambé, also gras-double (a tripe dish beloved locally but not by me); friendly atmosphere and service; menu 30–80F; rooms 40–90F.

Mont-de-Marsan – Le Midou, pl. Porte-Campet (58) 75.24.26: pretty rustic dining room with open wood fire; patron-chef Louis Bertrand cooks good family meals with large helpings, roast

Mont-de-Marsan is a strange town; it has a huge hippodrome for various horse shows, (trotting to show-jumping), a 'gentle' form of bull fighting without a bull being killed, only driven to despair, and a market for chickens and foie gras.

beef, kidneys in port, grills, roast duck, chicken; menu 50–75F; rooms 56–80F.

At Villeneuve-de-Marsan, 7km from Mont-de-Marsan – L'Europe (58) 75.20.08: rich food in regional style; good 60F menu; others 130–180F; rooms 80–160F.

N124 Dax (50km)

Richelieu, ave Victor-Hugo (58) 90.05.78: absolute favourite of local people; meals tend to be cheap in Les Landes area and the 45F menu of the day here is a real bargain – described by one of France's leading gourmets as 'angelic'! 80F menu of regional dishes excellent, too. Uncomplicated cooking of good fresh ingredients. Pleasant old-inn décor; rooms 55–90F; shut Sun. eve., Mon. 1 Oct.–1 May. Feb.

Du Bois de Boulogne (1km by allée des Baignots) (58) 74.23.32: country restaurant by small lake among trees; good lady chef – true Cordon Bleu; local dishes. Menu 32, 80F; garden tables; shut Tues. eve.; Weds.; Oct. Imports and sells whisky.

An old spa, with radioactive hot springs used for treatment of rheumatism; mud baths too. Fine walks and parks by the river Adour. Dax was under English rule from Richard the Lionheart's reign until 1451. Here was born, in 1576, a peasant, Vincent de Paul, who became priest, galley slave in Tunisia, and father of modern hospitals. He started soup kitchens, too, when Paris and then the Lorraine were threatened with famine. He was canonised as a saint in 1737.

N124 N10 Bayonne (46km)

Restaurant Euzkalduna, rue Pannecau (59) 59.28.02: genuine Basque cooking; fish specialities; dishes such as chipirons (cuttlefish) in dark spicey sauce; tripotcha (veal sausage); piperade (spiced omelette of peppers, tomatoes, onions); Basque fish soup; baudroie (angler

Capital of the French Basques, it became English when Eleanor of Aquitaine married Henry II, and stayed so for three centuries; the Basque fleet fought alongside our navy. But it was the last place in France to hold out against Wellington. Place de la

Bayonne
continued

fish); grilled gambas; piballes (small fried eels) and fresh tunny and anchovies in season from fishing fleet at St Jean-de-Luz; Spanish Rioja wines from 18F; meals around 80F; shut Sun. eve.; Mon.; part July; part. Oct.

Biarritz – Fronton Hotel, ave Joffre (59) 23.09.49: and its modern attachment La Résidence are both comfortable, middle-priced; meals good value; menu 35–52F; rooms 150F; shut part March; mid Oct.–mid Nov.

Hôtel l'Océan, pl. Ste Eugénie (59) 24.03.27: genuine Basque dishes – chipirons, poulet Basquais (cooked with tomatoes, peppers – served with rice); duck confit; good fish; menu 45–90F; wines from 20F; rooms 130–250F.

Liberté is an excellent and attractive shopping centre, with arcades.

Bayonne is known for its cured ham, chocolates, Armagnac and salmon from the Adour river. A most attractive city with a lovely cathedral and an interesting museum of Basque culture. 8km away is the still elegant, though fading, resort of Biarritz, developed from a fishing village by Napoleon III for his Empress Eugénie, and beloved by our Edward VII. It gets crowded high season now. The Hôtel Palais is the original palace built by Napoleon III for Eugénie so that she could be as near as possible to her beloved Spain. I remember when it was crammed with film stars. Now it draws rich Spaniards. Biarritz is the surfing capital of Europe so bathing is fun but dangerous. So is the beachside casino.

N10 St Jean de
Luz (21km)

La Vieille Auberge, rue Tourasse (59) 26.19.61: unpretentious, attractive little auberge in same family 28 years; chef-patron Daniel Grand attracts local families; Basque–Landais dishes; very good value; superb fish from local fleet includes fresh sardines, tunny; try fish soup, also ttoro (Basque bouillabaisse with tomato, onion, garlic); moules; paella; wines from 20F; menu 46–68F; shut 2 Jan.–1 April; Weds. low season.

A charming resort and busy fishing port. St Jean sailors and fishermen are known all over the world; they first fished the Newfoundland Banks in 1520, and now have the biggest tuna fishing fleet in France; many old houses towards the port; in the Baroque St Jean-Baptiste Church, Louis XIV married Marie-Thérèse, and the door through which they passed has been closed ever since.

At Ciboure, 1km over river, (many good small fish restaurants here) – Arrantzaleak, chemin de Halage (59) 26.10.75: splendid fish from quayside market daily – turbot, langoustines; sardines; daurade; excellent non-fish dishes, too – jugged wild boar; duck; various good omelettes; guitarist in evening; menu 60F; shut Weds. except in summer; 15 Dec.–15 Jan.

D912 to Hendaye and Spanish border (11km)

Most people are so busy going backwards and forwards between Spain and France that they don't notice Hendaye's very pleasant beach, backed by magnolias, palms and mimosa, and pretty promenade.

Index

Names of hotels and restaurants appear in *italics*.